JAMES DEWOLF

and the

RHODE ISLAND SLAVE TRADE

JAMES DEWOLF
and the
RHODE ISLAND SLAVE TRADE

CYNTHIA MESTAD JOHNSON

Charleston London

THE
History
PRESS

Published by The History Press
Charleston, SC 29403
www.historypress.net

Front cover, top: Watercolor of the *Macdonough* by Jonathan Alger Jr. *Photo taken by author, with permission from the Bristol Historical and Preservation Society. Bottom*: Bristol harbor and town. This is a very large original painting, artist W.E. Howe, 1931. *Photo taken by author with permission from the Bristol Historical and Preservation Society.*

Back cover: James DeWolf. *Reverend Calbraith Perry, DeWolf Genealogy, 1902, with permission and rights owned by the Bristol Historical and Preservation Society.*

First published 2014

Manufactured in the United States

ISBN 978.1.62619.479.3

Library of Congress CIP data applied for.

Notice: The information in this book is true and complete to the best of our knowledge. It is offered without guarantee on the part of the author or The History Press. The author and The History Press disclaim all liability in connection with the use of this book.

This is dedicated to my dad.

It's the personal journey and the legacy that matter.

CONTENTS

Preface   9
Acknowledgements   11
Introduction   13

1. Murder on the High Seas   23
2. The Golden Rock   32
3. Laws and Economics   44
4. The Pious Brother   59
5. DeWolf's Nemesis   68
6. Indians and Kidnapping   75
7. Politics   84
8. Slave Trade Accelerates   92
9. Frustration with the Law   102
10. Slaves and Cuba   115

Epilogue. The Demise of a Slave Trader   127
Appendix. Slave Trade Laws   131
Notes   135
Bibliography   149
Index   157
About the Author   160

PREFACE

I once saw two beautiful children playing together. One was a fair white child; the other was her slave, and also her sister.[1]

J ames DeWolf, of Bristol, Rhode Island, was a nefarious and wealthy slave trader. As an infamous early figure in the American slave trade during the late eighteenth and early nineteenth centuries, DeWolf emerged as a major entity, rivaling the even more famous John Brown of Providence, Rhode Island. Yet this narrative remains undocumented in our nation's historical record. Throughout this book, I will show how DeWolf continued to prosper and pursue his trading ventures despite the increasing restrictions on the international trade imposed by the nation's new federal government. This Rhode Islander was able to evade the local and federal authorities by wielding power that he amassed through his central role in sustaining Bristol's economy. DeWolf, unlike other slave traders, was able to organize a vertically integrated empire from which he controlled all aspects of the business, ranging from insuring vessels to the transportation of kidnapped Africans and their sales in the United States, West Indies and Cuba. Not only did DeWolf own the enterprise and its ancillary divisions, but he also captained many of the voyages, which helped him become one of the largest contributors toward the perpetuation of enslaved people in our nation's history.

What was revealed within the archival records was DeWolf's calloused attitude toward the slave trade and his ability to manipulate the legal system. Outlining the state and federal restrictions on the international slave trade,

DeWolf found it increasingly difficult to control his destiny, so he became actively involved in politics. He served as a member of the House of Representatives in the state of Rhode Island for multiple terms and as a United States senator, going so far as to change his political affiliation from Federalist to Republican in support of Jefferson's quest for the White House.

This book has corrected the historical record regarding the prosecutable activities of James DeWolf. It will also enrich the understanding of the role played by New Englanders, particularly Rhode Islanders, in the transatlantic slave trade. The central role that the North played in the continuance of the international trade has, until recently, been basically unexplored. What is revealed is that slave traders from Rhode Island helped to prolong the illegal trade for the South.

When examining DeWolf, it is imperative to recognize that he personally extended the plight of the African race both domestically and internationally. What has been determined is that the motivation to allow the slavers of the state to continue was in part based on the principle that the local economy was dependent on this illegal industry. The reality remains that James DeWolf and his family continued to escape the law and carry out their business, even after the 1808 trade moratorium, while building their family empire. This book is an important historical contribution and reference point for future studies on the American slave trade during the colonial era of our nation.

ACKNOWLEDGEMENTS

This book could not have been fully accomplished without the collaborative efforts of many people. I am deeply thankful for the emotional, spiritual and financial investments that were made by everyone in my immediate family. But more importantly, everyone involved believed as deeply as I did in correcting the historical record.

I would like to thank the Bristol Historical and Preservation Society (BHPS), which was by far the largest contributor of information and unending support for the last four years. I have found that it will be difficult to properly thank Derwent Jean Riding, president, and her board for how they have supported this project.

I have developed lifelong friendships through this journey that have also made valuable contributions toward the realization of this book. In no particular order of importance because they have all bestowed their knowledge on this research, I would like to thank: Mark J. Prak, Esq.; Nancy Kougeus, archivist and Cuba travel partner; Nic Adams, New York archivist; Mary Millard, private collection and images; Christy Nadalin, consultant; Reverend Cecilia Perry and Dr. Matthew Perry, family genealogy; Janelle Temnick, web design and formatting; Mike Dolan, editing; Dr. Jill Watts, mentor; Ron Wetteroth, St. Eustatius historian and images; David Tebaldi, Cuba tour advisor; Tom DeWolf, James DeWolf Perry V, Nancy Abercrombie and Dana Gibson, family history; Reinhard Battcher III, BHPS curator; Claire Benson, BHPS historian, Cuba travel partner and Rhode Island landlord; Pam Meyer, Joan Roth and June Truitt, BHPS; Jim Connell, Robin

ACKNOWLEDGEMENTS

Tremblay and David Harrington, Linden Place; Louis Cirillo, town clerk, Town of Bristol; Bert Lippincott III, reference librarian and genealogist, Newport Historical Society; Katherine Fox, reference, Baker Library, Harvard Business School; and J.D. Kay, rights and reproductions manager, Rhode Island Historical Society. If I have neglected to list someone who has been a part of this journey, it is with pure and utter innocence on my part and should not be taken personally—my apologies.

It goes without saying that family is the most important thing in my life, so a heartfelt thank-you to my sons, Tim Clinton, digital technician, images, maps, tables and formatting, and Matt Clinton, editing and insightful historical input; to my incredible parents, Dr. Orv and Shirley Mestad; and, without question, to the most supportive and understanding husband, Bill Johnson.

Lastly, a message to Casey: I hope that you will continue to be steadfast in your inquisitiveness and never forget how much you are loved.

INTRODUCTION

Nothing can exceed the wickedness and folly which continue to rule there. All sense of character as well as of right have [sic] been obliterated.[2]
—*James Madison, on the state of Rhode Island*

For years, United States history traditionally recounted slavery as a primarily southern states' issue during the seventeenth, eighteenth and nineteenth centuries. The image of the northern states as a pristine and perfect environment filled with proactive abolitionists and religious antislavery activists had gone almost unchecked until the 1960s. Essentially, the national mythology had absolved the North from any responsibility for slavery. This changed during the civil rights era, when the complicated relationship between the North and slavery was once again addressed. The institution of slavery not only existed and died slowly in some parts of the North and New England, but Rhode Island's economy also thrived on it, participating fully in the international trade.[3]

By the mid-twentieth century, New England's involvement in the slave trade was once again being looked at. This is when the three most active slave-trading states—Massachusetts, New York and particularly Rhode Island—were revealed. It was at this juncture that historians began to acknowledge the human atrocities that occurred in the trade. The North, including New England, was seen as a key player, but the primary focus remained on the South.

The slave trade thrived in the United States during the late eighteenth and early nineteenth centuries. The South had created a substantial need for free labor, and merchants in New England became overwhelming and willing participants in the fulfillment of that need. The southern ports that were the most prolific in the distribution of slaves were primarily Savannah, Georgia, and Charleston, South Carolina.[4] Far above the Mason-Dixon line, the North had a geographical advantage in its ability to turn a profit without being noticed by authorities during an era when the trade was being restricted, with the widespread focus primarily on the South. Rhode Island's contribution toward the need for slaves in the South was of long-term importance to the economic stability of the state, particularly in the coastal towns of Newport and Bristol.

Addressing the cruel realities of the slave trade, and New England's involvement in it, reveals a brutally shocking story. Specifically addressing Rhode Island's role brings the scope of preoccupation to a more refined geographical area. The existence of the illegal slave trade as a form of economic support for the coastal town of Bristol in the state of Rhode Island merited further investigation. Isolating it to one man's history through the dissection of the how and why of his unapologetic success offers a new perspective on Rhode Island's involvement in the slave trade. It makes it personal, particularly with the knowledge that this one man, James DeWolf, achieved such high positions of power and wealth through the suffering of so many human beings. Despite his transgressions, DeWolf remained a powerful and influential figure for the remainder of his life, both politically and as a leader of the people in Bristol. The question that needed to be asked is why this one incredibly wealthy and powerful man, who had such tremendous influence in his community, state and, ultimately, with five sitting presidents, never truly received his place in American history, particularly concerning the details of his single-handed continuation of the slave trade in our nation.

DeWolf and his family merit an in-depth examination regarding their central involvement in the slave trade, their critical economic support of the local economy and their influence on American politics and law. Revealing DeWolf's role and influence in Rhode Island's slave trade will thereby correct the national mythology of many historians regarding the discerning New England state.

Many citizens from the tiny state were responsible, directly or indirectly, for the delivery of more than 106,000 slaves to the United States, primarily to the South, between the years 1650 and 1808. However, the actual number delivered to the South, the West Indies and Cuba after 1808 remains a mystery. The involvement of Rhode Island citizens in the slave trade was widespread and abundant.[5] For select Rhode Islanders, the commercial success that came with their participation in the trade yielded tremendous economic stability both for themselves and their communities.

Rhode Island had already passed a law designed to prohibit slavery. In 1652, this law should have ended slavery, but it went largely ignored or unenforced for more than 130 years. Lacking the resources to enforce the law resulted in Rhode Island's haughty Puritan neighbors dubbing the slaving state a "moral sewer."[6] During the eighteenth century and into the nineteenth century, Rhode Island slave traders purchased and sold more slaves than all other slavers in the United States. By 1750, Rhode Island was recognized as the nation's most active trading center for slaves.[7] In 1774, Newport was declared the most active city in the slave trade of any town on the continent.[8] From 1725 to the end of 1807, it can be proven that Rhode Island was the most important base for American carriers of African slaves.[9] While a number of Rhode Island families participated in the trade, including the famous Brown family of Providence, among the most successful was the DeWolf family.[10] Their longevity in the trade was predicated on the lasting participation of central figure James DeWolf, who did almost anything to continue amassing economic and political power.

The DeWolf story begins in 1744 with Simeon Potter, a Rhode Island slave trader who, by the age of twenty-four, held a captain's license allowing him to be a captain for hire. Potter was documented in the DeWolf family history as the "most contentious and ornery Bristolian in the colonial century, if not in the town's whole history."[11] DeWolf historians have accurately asserted that Potter's success in the Sugar Islands trade was based on slave trafficking. During one of his slaving voyages, Potter landed on the French Island of Guadeloupe in the West Indian chain and signed on an inexperienced but enthusiastic new crew member, seventeen-year-old Mark Anthony DeWolf. Although DeWolf's grandparents were born in Connecticut, they eventually immigrated to Guadeloupe, where Mark Anthony was raised with American traditions in the Christian church and trained to read and write in several languages, including his parents' native language of English. Potter took an immediate liking to Mark Anthony because of his extensive education. It was just what the captain, who was illiterate, needed—someone to read and write for him. In turn, Potter began to teach DeWolf the routes and bargaining techniques of the slave trade.[12]

Simeon Potter had a reputation as an infamous pirate and privateer, creatively ignoring the law beginning at a young age. While on one of his many voyages, he landed on Guiana in South America and raided the

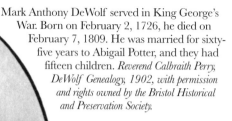

Mark Anthony DeWolf served in King George's War. Born on February 2, 1726, he died on February 7, 1809. He was married for sixty-five years to Abigail Potter, and they had fifteen children. *Reverend Calbraith Perry, DeWolf Genealogy, 1902, with permission and rights owned by the Bristol Historical and Preservation Society.*

Church of Oyapoc while he was there. At the time of the raid, Potter was twenty-four and captain of the *Prince Charles of Lorraine.* Father Fauque, from the parish, wrote to Bishop Kip, head of the diocese of that particular mission church. In his letter, he reported the incident and that Potter had stolen their sterling silver communion service. When Potter returned to Bristol, he gave the pillaged silver as a gift to St. Michael's Church in Bristol.[13]

The communion service was safely locked away during the civil rights era of the 1960s in response to the Watts Riots in Los Angeles, California, when elders of the church feared that Bristol, for some unforeseen reason, would also become a target of racial unrest. During this time, local churches began locking their doors and hiding their most valuable artifacts. The communion service is still locked away, perhaps because of its history, and remains unseen by the public today.[14]

Not too long after DeWolf began working for Potter, the captain took his young protégé home to Bristol and introduced him to his family, which included his nine sisters.[15] This resulted in a marriage between Mark Anthony and Potter's sister Abigail. The couple settled in Bristol, marking the beginning of the DeWolf legacy. Mark Anthony and Abigail had fifteen children; all eight of their sons went into the family business of human trafficking, and three died at sea. Of the five surviving DeWolf sons, James, born in 1764 and the second youngest, rose to become the family's most prominent slaver and businessman. Potter, who had such tremendous influence on Mark Anthony, also mentored the young James, teaching him the ruthless ways of his craft and how to circumvent the increasingly restrictive international legislation aimed at regulating slavers.[16] Potter's training and guidance regarding the slave trade was just one factor that helped to inspire DeWolf to build his empire.[17]

As the young United States grew, slaving began to undergo legal changes. James DeWolf sought to increase his political and economic influence by perpetuating the slave trade in the South from the New England port of Bristol. During his life, DeWolf attained significant political power and was eventually elected by voters in Rhode Island to their state's General Assembly. DeWolf served his state in political office almost uninterrupted from 1797 until the time of his death in 1837.[18] At the same time, while successfully circumventing slave laws both domestically and internationally, DeWolf maintained not only his lucrative business but also the family's lifestyle of wealth and power. A critical component of DeWolf's success undoubtedly had to do with his brilliant mind for entrepreneurialism and politics, as well as his immeasurable financial contribution to the local economy.

Bristol became economically dependent on DeWolf's success in human trafficking. This was perhaps the justification needed for local residents to turn a blind eye toward the realities of the DeWolfs' involvement. There were unlimited financial possibilities for locals that far exceeded the limited agricultural land and sparse factory work. But DeWolf did not attain success without continual challenges and roadblocks, particularly those placed in his path by the man who would later emerge as his nemesis, Rhode Island customhouse collector William Ellery.

On January 1, 1808, the Federal Slave Trade Act was implemented with the intention of putting an end to all slave importations to the United States or its territories. This law stated that the importation of slaves into the United States or its territories was banned and increased the penalties for infractions.[19] This was a critical law for the nation, as previous state and federal slave laws had been readily ignored. However, DeWolf's success continued up to and well beyond 1808, despite the passage of the act and its extensive penalties for its violation. As a private citizen and a politician sworn to uphold the federal laws of the United States, DeWolf continued to purchase and traffic in slaves well beyond the federally mandated deadline.

Bristol, Rhode Island, remains a quaint seaport village today with myriad original buildings and homes that were constructed during DeWolf's lifetime using the proceeds from the slave trade. Many of the families, including the DeWolfs, led risky and adventuresome lives as they sailed the Seven Seas, lived in tropical climates and brought home the most exotic products garnered from their worldwide trading. The town was so committed to the seafaring trade that the main roads leading to the wharves at the harbor's edge were built twice as wide as any other streets in town and remain as such today. This was to accommodate the many wagons that carried cargo to and from the multiple vessels moored in Bristol Harbor. The extra-wide

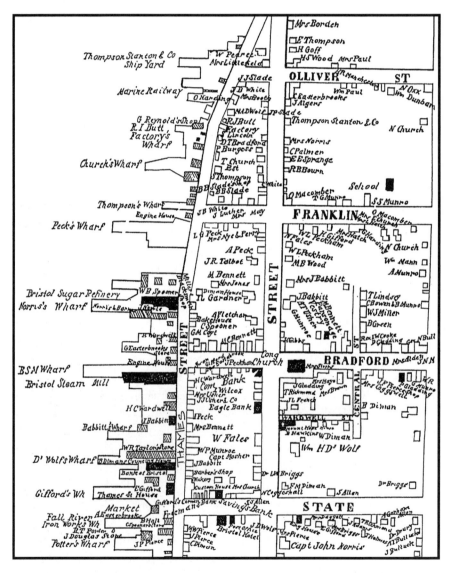

Pencil sketch of the town of Bristol, circa 1851. *Provided by the Bristol Historical and Preservation Society.*

Linden Place, built by General George DeWolf. Uncle James DeWolf begrudgingly paid part of his nephew's debt so he would not lose this magnificent home. *Photo taken by author.*

The Linden Place staircase climbs four stories in this beautiful Russell Warren architectural design. *Reverend Calbraith Perry, DeWolf Genealogy, 1902, with permission and rights owned by the Bristol Historical and Preservation Society.*

streets were named Franklin, Bradford and, the closest to the DeWolf wharf, State. The two streets that run parallel to the harbor are quite a bit narrower and have the typical New England names of Thames, closest to the water, and Hope, one block to the east. Hope Street is lined with mature trees that shade most of the original architecture of the town, including Linden Place, a majestic Federal-style home designed by Russell Warren and once owned by DeWolf's nephew George. Warren's recognizable architectural designs are prevalent throughout this coastal town. One of the characteristics of Bristol from the 1790s would be the number of new buildings, as the town was virtually destroyed during the American Revolution. The wealth that abounded locally as a result of the slave trade enabled this quaint seaport to be restored quickly.

There is a town common three blocks from the harbor where the original burial ground once stood, but it has since been moved. Not too far from the town common is a neighborhood referred to as New Gorée. This was the area in Bristol where freed slaves established their residence after the local abolition of slavery. It is very telling that the newly freed slaves chose to name their neighborhood after Gorée Island, which is located off the coast of Africa. This island was used as a holding area for slaves who were imprisoned there until they made their journey across the Atlantic Ocean at the hands of their captors.

The people of Bristol have an expanded knowledge of the history of their town, homes and buildings. Many of the homes in the original village that were built in the late eighteenth and early nineteenth centuries still have descendants living in them, being passed down from generation to generation. The families who live in homes unrelated to their heritage have knowledge of the lineage—who built them and what professions former residents were engaged in at the time of construction. Many were in the business of smuggling contraband goods or slave trading, which funded the building of these magnificent residences. There is a beautiful house built by one of the many sea captains that has a tunnel that was once accessed from inside the home and stretched the length of the yard to the bay. Within the tunnel, now closed off from reaching the water, remain some hogsheads once used in a previous life.

It was here that James DeWolf was born on March 18, 1764, to Mark Anthony and Abigail Potter DeWolf. Both parents were members of St. Michael's Episcopal Church in Bristol, located on Hope Street, where they baptized most of their children. But by the time Abigail had her sixth son, William, she had shifted her membership to the Congregational Church

Hogsheads used for carrying rum and other supplies found in a secret tunnel that leads to the edge of Bristol Harbor, circa 1800s. *Photo taken by author.*

on High Street, where her last four surviving children, including James, were baptized. Abigail's children were married in the Congregational Church, and the wives of her sons became members. However, there is no record of active membership in either church by James DeWolf or any of his slaving brothers.[20]

The overarching success of DeWolf, his brothers and their extended family can be examined by simply walking the streets of Bristol today. Bristol residents are deeply embedded in the history of their town, and the folklore

James DeWolf, boy soldier during the American Revolution, became a captain before age twenty, married Nancy Ann Bradford on January 7, 1790, and fathered eleven children. Reverend Calbraith Perry, DeWolf Genealogy, 1902, with permission and rights owned by the Bristol Historical and Preservation Society.

is passed from generation to generation. Stories are often altered through time with colorful embellishments, but most telling of the truth remains in letters, ledgers and legal documents miraculously preserved in basements or attics and subsequently forgotten. As the puzzle pieces begin to come together, DeWolf's life formulates a clear picture of his unyielding nature and the advancements he contributed in sustaining the illegal slave trade in our nation.

Chapter 1

MURDER ON THE HIGH SEAS

*Failing to serve an arrest warrant for murder, Marshal William Peck of Rhode
Island stated, "DeWolf could not by me be found."*[21]

James DeWolf of Bristol, Rhode Island, sailed from Africa to Havana,
Cuba, in 1790 on his ship the *Polly* with a new load of slaves. As an
experienced captain, DeWolf had knowledge of navigation, the possibilities
of bad weather, the danger of encountering pirates and the potential for
illness among the crew and the human cargo.[22] Early on in the voyage, one of
the slaves, a middle-aged woman, became ill with smallpox. DeWolf decided
to quarantine her on the top deck, away from the rest of the slaves, to avoid
infecting the ship's population. To ensure that his crew was not exposed
to her illness, DeWolf ordered that the slave be tied to a chair to keep her
from wandering about. It has been speculated that there was not actually
a chair on board but that perhaps the slave was sequestered to the crow's
nest, a basket or seat often made of webbing, usually with leg holes, attached
to the top of the center mast of a vessel. Seamen used the crow's nest to
spot land or oncoming vessels. However, while a bird's nest was hoisted up
and down the center mast, rarely was it removable. It was reported that
DeWolf noticed that the slave, still tied to some form of chair, had rapidly
deteriorated. He then made the determination that she needed to be killed.[23]

Initially, DeWolf asked for a volunteer to carry out the task of murder, and
according to a deposition from the court, the entire crew refused, telling him
that they would have nothing to do with it.[24] DeWolf then ordered a crew

member to draw down a hoist with the grappling hook and assist him with the device. A gag was tied around the slave woman's mouth to silence her and ensure that if she screamed for help, the other slaves below deck would not hear her.[25] DeWolf then gave a new command to help him with the hoist. The hook was placed into the rope at the back of the chair, and the woman was lifted into the air. It was then that DeWolf swung her over the side of the ship, dropping her into the sea—alive. Toward the end of the deposition, crew members claimed that once DeWolf had dropped the woman into the sea, he stated how sorry he was to have lost such a good chair.[26]

Once the voyage ended and the *Polly* returned to port in Rhode Island, DeWolf created his account of sales for his cargo of slaves. On it, he meticulously listed each slave and the price he had collected for them individually. At the bottom of his ledger, DeWolf noted that 109 slaves were sold for profit. Additionally, a boy was given to someone whose name is illegible. DeWolf personally kept 10 slaves, 1 male slave was infirm at the conclusion of the voyage and 1 female slave was noted to have died during the voyage. DeWolf clearly had no compulsion to hide the fact that, indeed, a death on the voyage had occurred.[27]

Simultaneously, after the *Polly* returned to Rhode Island, someone—it is not clear whom—reported the incident to the local authorities. However, it has been speculated that it was federally appointed customs collector from Newport William Ellery, as he had become acutely aware of DeWolf's slaving practices and wanted desperately to see them end.[28]

As collector, William Ellery had a multitude of responsibilities, which included, among other things, upholding maritime laws, inspections of vessels as they arrived and departed, crew inspections, verification of insurance policies and measurements of all vessels to determine their tonnage. He was acutely aware of the guidelines of each slave law as it was implemented, and he maintained communication with the Department of Treasury in Washington, D.C., which saw that the laws were carried out for the president. As seen through a lifetime of correspondence, Ellery took his position as collector very seriously.[29]

Surprisingly, the persistent and law-abiding Ellery came from a similar family background as DeWolf. He grew up in a home where slaving constituted the family's livelihood in the mid-eighteenth century. William Ellery Sr. was involved in the slave trade for years. However, his son and namesake came to abhor the trade and chose to follow a different route. He became an antislavery activist and was deeply involved in the political development of the early United States.

Slave ledger from the *Polly*. At the bottom, DeWolf noted that he kept ten slaves for himself and acknowledged the death of the female slave he threw overboard. *Provided by Bristol Historical and Preservation Society.*

Ellery was a representative of Rhode Island at the Continental Congress and one of the signers of the Declaration of Independence. In 1790, George Washington appointed him the collector for the customhouse in Newport. Ellery remained in the position of collector until his death in 1820 at the age of ninety-two. He exhibited extraordinary determination as he fulfilled the duties of collector, struggling through many political differences with several administrations, as well as with the DeWolf family.

At the first session of the federal grand jury in Rhode Island on June 15, 1791, a court deposition was taken from two of DeWolf's crew members from the *Polly*. Thomas Gorton and Jonathon Cranston recounted what they saw regarding the plight of the African woman.[30]

According to the deposition taken from the two crewmen, the woman suffering from smallpox was brought above deck and tied to a chair by both DeWolf and Gorton. The crewmen stated that she received some water to drink, with the crew paying only marginal attention to her for fear of contracting this highly infectious disease. After two days of being tied to a chair and exposed to the elements, it was noted that she became increasingly ill, according to both Gorton's and Cranston's accounts. Captain DeWolf called his crew together and determined that the slave needed to be thrown overboard in order to protect not only his valuable slave cargo but also everyone on the ship. He made no effort to help her first. The deposition concluded with the following summary of DeWolf's alleged crime:

> [DeWolf] *not having the fear of God before his eyes, but being moved and seduced by the instigation of the Devil…did feloniously, willfully and of his malice aforethought, with his hands clinch and seize in and upon the body of said Negro woman…and did push, cast and throw her from out of said vessel into the Sea and waters of the Ocean, whereby and whereupon she then and there instantly sank, drowned and died.*[31]

Abolitionist sentiment had risen in the years following the American Revolution. Rhode Island's Gradual Emancipation Act of 1784, which was written to stop both slavers and slaveholders from exhibiting a cruel and blatant disregard for human beings, attacked the attitude that slaves were just property. Both the Federal Slave Trade Act of 1784, which declared that no American should be engaged in the slave trade, and the Rhode Island Act of 1787, which stated that no slave was to be imported into the state of Rhode Island, were broken by DeWolf.[32]

Moreover, in 1790, just prior to DeWolf's offense, the first Federal Crimes Act had passed, making it a federal offense to commit murder or other crimes on the high seas. It gave jurisdiction to the federal courts to deal directly with violators of federal laws and included no exceptions for slaveholders or slave traders. DeWolf's crime was recognized by the federal government as an act of piracy and murder on the high seas and, if he were found guilty through a trial by jury, was punishable by death. Although DeWolf never faced a trial on U.S. soil, if he had, he would have been charged, at the very minimum, with manslaughter. According to the Federal Act of 1790, manslaughter, too, was punishable by death, whether the act was committed on land or at sea, within the United States maritime boundaries or outside of them.[33] Whether collector Ellery was involved in the *Polly* case, he would not have objected to DeWolf's prosecution as a result of the deposition because DeWolf had positively broken the law, and Ellery was acutely aware of that fact.[34]

Slaves were considered by slave traders and slaveholders as chattel, pieces of personal or real property owned by individuals. Yet the willful killing of slaves was illegal. However, these crimes were rarely, if ever, prosecuted within the states because state legal codes provided exceptions that allowed slave owners to claim that the killing of the slave had been justified or accidental. Slave captains routinely ordered crew members to throw sick slaves overboard, almost as a matter of hygiene, to keep them from contaminating the cargo and, more importantly, the crew.[35] Since captains often asserted that they had the right to end the life of a sick or rebellious slave, for some it remained difficult to understand why DeWolf was charged with murder. Nevertheless, the law remained on the side of the slave.

The federal grand jury in Rhode Island found DeWolf guilty and charged him with violation of a federal law. Attorney General John Jay, under the direction of President Washington, submitted the request for the arrest of DeWolf on the charge of murder. A warrant was then issued for DeWolf's seizure. The deposition that justified the warrant was taken on Wednesday, June 15, 1791. The date of the warrant's dissemination would have occurred between Thursday, June 16, and Friday, June 24, 1791. Although it had been less than ten days since the crew members gave their deposition, DeWolf could not be found. Shortly after the warrant was given to the marshal for DeWolf's seizure, a brief article appeared in the *Providence Gazette* on June 25, 1791, that addressed DeWolf's murder charge. It stated:

> *The Grand Jury found a bill against James DeWolf of Bristol, in this State, for the willful murder of a Negro Woman on a late* [African]

Guinea Voyage. There was not a trial on this bill as Capt. DeWolf had quitted [departed] *the United States immediately after his arrival from the said voyage.*[36]

A couple of months prior to DeWolf's impending arrest, the deputy marshal of Rhode Island placed an announcement in the *Newport Herald* declaring that, on behalf of Rhode Island's district court judge Henry Marchant and William Ellery, a warrant had been granted for a vessel from Bristol that broke the 1790 federal law. The vessel had been seized, and the captain and crew were set to go on trial for carrying onboard items for the sole purpose of participating in the purchasing and selling of slaves.[37] The publication of such occurrences had become more prevalent in local newspapers, perhaps as an aggressive reminder that Ellery had the support of local and federal officials regarding enforcement of the law.

The first federally appointed local marshal, William Peck, reported to the Rhode Island federal court system semiannually that he continued to attempt to serve the arrest warrant for four years, from 1791 until 1795, but that he could not find DeWolf.[38] Bristolian legend states that no one seemed to know where DeWolf had disappeared to during his four-year absence, or at least no one was willing to admit to knowledge of his whereabouts. How was legal justice so easily evaded? Who was James DeWolf, and how was he able to successfully orchestrate a system that allowed this to happen? Did DeWolf create the conditions that allowed him the freedom to not only commit murder but also to evade arrest? For the time being, DeWolf had managed to elude the authorities while he continued to build his family empire from afar. However, was Peck party to the murkiness regarding DeWolf's whereabouts?

This is where the family trees of Bristolian residents begin to intertwine. It also alludes to the reason DeWolf was "never found." Marshal Peck's paternal uncle was a captain in the slave trade. Peck's cousin by his paternal uncle, Elizabeth Peck, was married to Samuel Bosworth, who was under William Ellery's employ as the local surveyor for the port of Bristol/Warren. Elizabeth's brother Nicholas Peck was also a slave captain who had a son in the business. Nicholas's son married Ann Bradford, the niece of Nancy Bradford DeWolf, who happened to be the wife of James DeWolf. Nicholas Jr. and Ann named their firstborn son William DeWolf Peck. Nicholas Jr. was also hired by DeWolf to captain his ship the *Nancy*, which originally carried ninety slaves onboard but delivered only seventy-five in Havana.[39] The complicated family tree of DeWolf shows that he was related by marriage to both the marshal's family and the family of the surveyor for

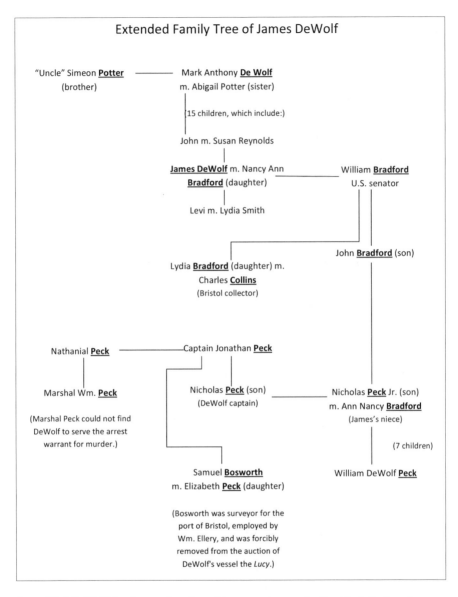

Extended Family Tree of James DeWolf

"Uncle" Simeon **Potter** —— Mark Anthony **De Wolf**
(brother)   m. Abigail Potter (sister)

(15 children, which include:)

John m. Susan Reynolds

James DeWolf m. Nancy Ann   William **Bradford**
Bradford (daughter)   U.S. senator

Levi m. Lydia Smith

John **Bradford** (son)

Lydia **Bradford** (daughter) m.
Charles **Collins**
(Bristol collector)

Nathanial **Peck** —— Captain Jonathan **Peck**

Marshal Wm. **Peck**   Nicholas **Peck** (son)   Nicholas **Peck** Jr. (son)
      (DeWolf captain)   m. Ann Nancy **Bradford**
(Marshal Peck could not find   (James's niece)
DeWolf to serve the arrest
warrant for murder.)   (7 children)

Samuel **Bosworth**   William DeWolf **Peck**
m. Elizabeth **Peck** (daughter)

(Bosworth was surveyor for the
port of Bristol, employed by
Wm. Ellery, and was forcibly
removed from the auction of
DeWolf's vessel the *Lucy*.)

A modified DeWolf family tree that shows his connections to the Bradford, Peck and Bosworth families. *Table created for the author by Tim Clinton.*

the port of Bristol. Both men were keenly aware of the efficacious means of which DeWolf was capable.

Since a slaver's insurance covered the mortality of slaves at a predetermined percentage rate of anywhere between 5 to 25 percent, it was not uncommon

A Bristol Insurance Company receipt signed by James DeWolf. Signers would tear out a portion of their name to denote that the balance was paid in full. *Photo taken by author, with permission from the Bristol Historical and Preservation Society.*

for captains to throw overboard a mortally ill or deceased slave to protect the rest of the human cargo and crew from infection. Insurance policies written for slaving vessels stated that payment for the mortality of "black cargo" would not be honored unless the loss of a predetermined percentage of slaves had been documented.[40] For example, an insurance policy established that a captain could collect on a policy if 25 percent of his cargo died. If a captain lost a small number of slaves to disease, it would not be cost effective for him to throw additional slaves overboard in order to file an insurance claim. Instead, the captain would take every precaution to maintain the health of the remainder of his cargo, as the sale of the slaves yielded a higher profit margin than the payment from an insurance policy unless the entire vessel was lost.

Bristolian commerce depended on the success of the DeWolf family. The seaport of Bristol, located in a prime location on Narragansett Bay, made the town's transition to a seafaring community quite easy. With several natural inlets and harbors throughout the state, a number of vessels came and went with ease. Along with the shipping industry came employment for Bristolians both as crew members and longshoremen. DeWolf's business enterprises helped fuel the town's rapid transition, and Bristol quickly became dependent on the shipping industry, which predominantly involved the slave trade.[41]

However, amid the growing success of his business ventures, DeWolf encountered a serious impediment: he was charged with murdering a slave. This was an unusual accusation, as it was well known that captains of slaving vessels executed slaves with impunity.[42] Perhaps he was already being targeted as an example because of his visibility. It also outlines the vulnerability of a man who was in the midst of building an empire that undoubtedly would have inspired his decision to go into politics.

Chapter 2

THE GOLDEN ROCK

While it was considered a criminal offense to willfully kill a slave, there was never any compulsion in the West Indies to attach a heavy penalty.[43]

DeWolf's family maintained discretion in regards to his whereabouts at the time of and following his disappearance. But indeed they did know where he was, and their correspondence with him revealed that he had fled to St. Eustatius Island in the West Indies. DeWolf could have gone to any number of locations. He was familiar with Spanish-controlled Cuba, where he was known to conduct business, but he might have feared that would be a logical place for authorities to seek him. His father was a Dutch native of Guadeloupe Island in the West Indies, where DeWolf might also have been welcomed. Instead, he chose the Dutch island of St. Eustatius, known as "Statia," just north of Guadeloupe and next to St. Thomas on the northeast corner of the West Indian chain.[44] Perhaps DeWolf made this choice because the residents were fluent in English. But more likely, he selected Statia because it was a considerably active slave depot, one he had visited before.[45]

Statia presented certain lawful opportunities favorable to DeWolf as well. During the late eighteenth century, the legal responsibilities of a governor in the Dutch West Indies were exceedingly broad. Although there was an elected assembly, the authority over each island lay solely in the hands of the governor, who had a wide range of obligations, including sitting as head of the highest court of appeals in all civil matters. Essentially, governors

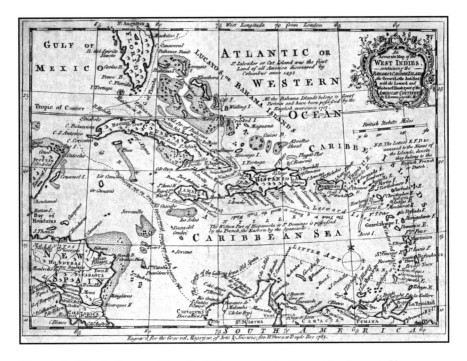

Map of the West Indies containing the Bahamas and Caribbean Islands created by Emanuel Bowen. *Courtesy of the Library of Congress, digital call number, 2010593325.*

remained entirely free from restraint while carrying out governmental and legal affairs in any manner they deemed appropriate.[46] It was the epitome of a good old boys club.

West Indian law recognized the slave trade as legal and considered all slaves as personal property or chattel. While it was a criminal offense to willfully kill a slave, there was never any compulsion in the West Indies to attach a heavy penalty. Any attempt to protect slaves in the West Indies went largely ignored. In Statia, residents were so ambivalent regarding the laws written specifically to protect slaves that they lacked a willingness to recognize that the deliberate killing of a slave was an act of homicide or murder.[47] This overarching attitude toward slaves would support the contention that DeWolf did nothing wrong when he made the decision to throw the slave overboard to her death, at least in the West Indies.

In the late eighteenth century, the thriving sugar market in Europe facilitated the spread of sugar production, resulting in an equally high demand for slaves. The West Indies were a transitional stop before the last leg of a journey, and after sailing through the grueling Middle Passage, they were

Aerial view of the active port of St. Eustatius in the northern Leeward Islands of the West Indies, circa 177?, artist unknown. *Courtesy of Library of Congress, digital call number 2012590109.*

a practical location for fulfilling the need for slaves in order to accommodate the mass production of sugar commodities for the world market. Sugar had become the most essential product of European capitalism, actualizing competitive maritime power.[48] This resulted in an overarching attitude of leniency toward all international slave trade laws and a motivating factor for DeWolf to choose the island of Statia as his temporary hiding place.[49] Statia, by law, required all captains or owners of vessels who transported goods, including slaves, to the island to apply for permits once they landed.[50] Upon his arrival, DeWolf applied for and was granted a permit. This gave him the status of burgher (citizen) and allowed him to trade legally from the port of Statia.[51]

By 1757, Statia had already garnered the nickname the "Golden Rock," which referred to its thriving port and free trade.[52] On any given day by the mid-1770s, as many as twenty ships from the United States crowded into the port of Statia. The governor during that time, Johannes de Graaf, personally owned one-quarter of the island and more than four hundred slaves. As governor, he made very little money. However, his involvement in Statia's trade port yielded him more than sixty times the amount of his annual salary in additional revenue.[53] Statia relied heavily on the outside world for the island's commerce since it had no natural resources to sustain its population; islanders survived on subsistence farming, animal husbandry and fishing. The land was barren and could not support large-scale agriculture. Trade was vitally important for survival of this tiny island of less than seven square miles.[54] Its attitude of neutrality toward all countries that traded on the island helped to establish Statia as the "supermarket for the world," particularly in the business of trading slaves, and American ships were welcomed without reserve.[55] Not only was Statia a free port, charging no import or export taxes, but it also had storehouse facilities to hold slaves and was in a key market location within the transatlantic trade. Islands surrounding Statia were controlled by English, French, Danish and Spanish colonies, all of which actively traded at Statia's port.[56] The island was different from the others in the West Indies as it maintained a consistent position of neutrality, making it advantageous to all nations and an emporium to the world.[57] This was an economically lucrative decision for the entire island.

While past governors had been sympathetic to the slave trade, Governor de Graaf had a copious personal involvement that set the tone for future governors by openly extending the island to slavers. He maintained his supportive position regarding slavery and the slave trade throughout his

A slave register for St. Eustatius, written in Dutch. It seems malicious to place a heart around the title of a slave-accounting ledger. *Photo courtesy of Ron Wetteroth, private collection.*

tenure, setting a precedent for future governors to do the same. As a result of Statia's reputation as a slave depot, many merchants were drawn to the island, settling temporarily and given the title of "transient" by the locals.[58] In 1787, Johannes Runnels replaced de Graaf as the new governor of Statia. Runnels, a defrocked minister and a descendant of one of the oldest families on the island, commonly accepted bribes to ignore the island's laws and was regarded by locals as incompetent. Runnels's position required him to govern three islands: St. Eustatius, St. Maarten and Saba.[59] By the late eighteenth century, despite his controversial leadership, Runnels had ensured that Statia evolved into a significant port in the West Indies, particularly for slave traders.[60] This set the stage for DeWolf to continue his profitable business of buying and selling slaves without drawing too much attention.

During DeWolf's four-year hiatus from Bristol, there were nineteen known slaving voyages on his vessels.[61] The ambitious nature of DeWolf's entrepreneurial spirit could not be squelched as a result of his sequestration in the West Indies. Additionally, he regularly corresponded with his brother John, primarily regarding personal financial matters. James, a seemingly devoted husband and father, instructed John on how his household in Bristol should be run and how to care for his wife and family during his extended absence. John's signature, found on ledgers from general stores in Bristol for documentation of financial responsibility, read: "James DeWolf, by John DeWolf."[62] Interestingly, everything was paid for in cash despite the availability of credit to the DeWolfs. Of the many DeWolf brothers, John and the two youngest sons, James and Levi, were particularly close. When it came to business, they meticulously wrote everything down, even if it was a small item or insignificant amount of money, demonstrating their strong business sense and accountability to one another. Their personal accounts were always reconciled in tedious detail, and at times, the IOU's were written on the smallest slips of paper.[63] Thus, older brother John signed his name on all accounts that he personally handled on behalf of his brother James.[64]

If not for the constant devotion and commitment by both younger brother Levi and older brother John to James, the family's income that James had so diligently established might have been severely damaged during his absence. As a result, John and Levi, who helped to perpetuate the family's role in the slave trade, are just as responsible as James for the involuntary imprisonment of so many Africans.

While James DeWolf continued to direct his family business from Statia, Isaac Manchester, a Rhode Island slave trade captain for hire, learned of the pending warrant against DeWolf in Bristol.[65] Manchester became aware of where DeWolf was hiding, traveled to the West Indies and reported the crime of murder to judge advocate Christian Petri regarding the incident on the *Polly*.[66] What motivation could possibly have enticed this man to report a crime that was pending in the United States? Manchester was not DeWolf's competitor, at least not directly. Manchester was a captain for hire who did not own his own ship. Allegedly, Manchester was nothing more than an opportunist looking for personal financial gain. Given that Manchester later captained ships for the DeWolfs, there is a possibility that James was the mastermind behind Manchester's visit to the island, or perhaps this is an example of keep your friends close and your enemies closer. One thing is certain: Manchester was not on the fateful voyage of the *Polly* when the tragic incident took place.[67] Although it would have been risky, there is even the plausibility that the family strategy was to push for a trial in the West Indies in an attempt to convince the prosecutor in Rhode Island that the evidence was in DeWolf's favor and that the charges for murder should be dropped.

Subsequently, Judge Perti notified DeWolf of Manchester's complaint and placed the slaver on trial in the West Indies. On August 8, 1792, James wrote a letter to his brother Levi, primarily giving him more directions on running the family business, as well as instructions for his brother's next voyage to Africa. But in the middle of this extremely long letter, DeWolf made reference to a letter that he wrote to Judge John Jay in Washington, D.C., that was personally delivered by his father-in-law, Senator Bradford of Rhode Island. In speaking of this to Levi, he expressed his disappointment in not receiving a response from Judge Jay, as he had written a letter of apology regarding the incident on the *Polly*. Apparently, DeWolf was hopeful for federal intervention regarding the warrant for his arrest. Simultaneously, at the time the letter was written to Jay, DeWolf instructed a newly named vessel to set sail on July 4 from Bristol on a voyage to purchase slaves. The DeWolf sloop was aptly named *Judge Jay*.[68]

Knowing the probability of a trial in the West Indies for his accusation of murder was imminent, DeWolf asked Levi to contact three or four specific crew members to come to Statia immediately. In the letter, DeWolf suggested Isaac Stockman as one possibility and requested that Levi find additional willing participants. There were people in Bristol who would make themselves available for DeWolf and for job security. DeWolf had carefully chosen men he could trust to be used as character witnesses on his behalf. He suggested a couple modes of travel, all of which would be on DeWolf ships, explaining that the men would easily arrive in Statia before the trial was to begin.[69]

Stockman and another sailor, Henry Claning, were both natives of Newport and traveled to Statia at the request of DeWolf. Although DeWolf specifically requested the presence of Stockman for help with the new deposition, no evidence confirms that either Stockman or Claning had actually sailed on the *Polly*. Once on the island, Stockman and Claning were registered and classified as transients since neither man was a documented resident of Statia.[70] The two men stayed and remained in DeWolf's employ, on call for the impending trial. This created a lucrative opportunity for DeWolf to help his crew members remember exactly what happened on the *Polly*, even if they were not on the original voyage, and to rehearse their testimony. Regardless of whether or not Stockman and Claning were on the vessel in question, these two men were vital to DeWolf in achieving his ultimate goal: to be found innocent of the charge of murder.

A legal document from the customhouse in Newport giving permission for the sloop *Judge Jay*, owned by DeWolf, to depart from the Rhode Island port destined for St. Croix. *Photo taken by author, with permission from the Bristol Historical and Preservation Society.*

On June 15, 1794, Stockman and Claning were interviewed, and yet another deposition was submitted regarding the incident on the *Polly*. Slave ship owners commonly bribed crew members, often for their continued loyalty and discretion regarding illegal slaving matters, and this was likely in DeWolf's case.[71] Isaac Stockman and Henry Claning stated in the deposition that they worked as crew members on the *Polly* for DeWolf in 1791.[72] They gave their accounts of what happened to the slave woman onboard the *Polly* for this new deposition, with the core of the story remaining the same. Only this time, the description carried an obvious compassionate undertone regarding Captain DeWolf. He was described as a sensitive and concerned human being, not only for his crew but for the suffering slave as well.

Stockman and Claning stated in the new deposition that it was an unfortunate situation they had onboard and that the crew was apprehensive about their own personal safety. The sailors further declared that DeWolf had no alternative but to save the crew and cargo, which consisted of 142 slaves and 15 crew members, 10 of whom reportedly had never contracted smallpox and therefore had no natural immunity to the disease, although there is no verifiable truth to this statement. Since they further declared that it did not appear that the woman would recover, she was, without malice, thrown overboard. Finally, Stockman and Claning stated that DeWolf and the crew were equally sickened by the circumstances that compelled them to adopt this disagreeable solution.[73] The first deposition stated that the crew wanted nothing to do with ending the woman's life. But the newfound declaration of DeWolf's compassion in the second deposition presents an entirely different scenario.

The crewmen maintained in the second deposition that the female slave, seated on the top deck, remained there for three to four days, not two as stated in the first deposition. Stockman and Claning also insisted that the female slave received constant medical care and attention, which was the opposite of what was originally stated in the deposition taken in Rhode Island. In the first deposition, two crew members who were actually present on the fated voyage swore under oath that the woman was given very little water and nothing else.

Most slave voyages during this time period did not employ physicians. Holding the woman above deck would have made her far more ill due to extended exposure, but placing her below the hold would risk infecting the other slaves. The second deposition clearly differed from the first as it stated the female slave was given constant medical care, a blanket for warmth and food and water and had succumbed—or at least nearly so—by the time she was thrown overboard after much debate and consternation. It made no mention of the woman being gagged or tied to a chair or that DeWolf threw her overboard with the callous comment that he was sorry he had lost such a good chair.[74]

The deposition taken in the West Indies stated that the crew thought the female slave might have already died by the time she was "humanely" thrown overboard.[75] The second deposition neglected to mention that the first deposition spoke of a gag tied around the woman's mouth to keep her from making a sound. Clearly, a gag would not be needed if the woman was, in fact, already dead or nearly so. The nature of the slave's mortality in the second deposition is replete with incessant and intentional vagueness.

Governor Runnels was the only witness to the deposition; Judge Petri was not present. It is not known if one of Runnels's responsibilities as governor was to be an official witness to legal proceedings. Perhaps in this case, Runnels was a willing witness for the right financial arrangement, particularly when one considers his damaged character. Runnels had the reputation on the island for being open to many forms of bribery. It also appeared that DeWolf had personally laid out the ideal situation for a successful trial. With Stockman's and Claning's testimonies, a more compassionate tale was woven for DeWolf's defense in the second deposition.[76]

The environment on Statia would have been friendly, one in which a second deposition could be easily defended. Once the deposition was witnessed and recorded by Runnels, he delivered the cleverly crafted document to Judge Petri of St. Thomas ,where the trial was to be held.[77] St. Thomas governed itself similarly to Statia in that it had an economy built by merchants and planters who participated in the slave trade. Many Statia merchants, including expatriates, relocated to the island of St. Thomas, which is three times larger than Statia with a much larger port and available land.

Not feeling threatened by his sequestration, DeWolf continued to conduct business from afar for two more years. While he maintained an active role in his lucrative business transporting hundreds of slaves, the trial was finally set to begin. James wrote to his brother John on August 8, 1794:

> As you are going to England [to sell sugar]…meet me…you will not I hope fail to write to me by all opportunity from England on where you may be, that I may the better govern myself how to proceed and when and where I shall meet you in the West Indies…give me the earliest notice possible.[78]

As demonstrated through regular correspondence, DeWolf relied heavily on his brothers not only for the continuance of his business enterprises, but also, with a trial pending, he might have depended on their emotional support as well.

On April 29, 1795, the judge reviewed the deposition to determine whether a trial should be held for the murder of a slave.[79] After speaking with Manchester, DeWolf's handpicked witnesses, supposed crew members and, finally, DeWolf himself, the judge absolved the slave captain of any wrongdoing and dismissed the charges for the crime of murdering the slave woman.[80] Although the judge stated that he initially felt DeWolf was cruel, committing an act of wanton barbarity, and morally evil, the judge was ultimately moved by DeWolf's actions to save the lives of his crew. The judge even implied that he felt DeWolf did the honorable thing to save his men and had been convinced by witnesses that he did everything in his power to help the poor slave woman.[81]

As a result of the undoubtedly well-rehearsed second deposition and testimonies of Stockman and Claning, the charges for murder against DeWolf were dropped in the West Indies. If DeWolf did, in fact, orchestrate this entire scenario, he not only must have had a good working knowledge of West Indian law regarding the charges brought against him but also felt confident that the good old boy court system of St. Thomas would find him innocent.[82] However, DeWolf most likely was presented with an unplanned situation that once again threatened his freedom and possibly his life. DeWolf either crafted a scenario in which he personally benefitted or had the ability to manipulate the positive outcome.

Why St. Eustatius was willing to involve itself in prosecuting a man for murder while a proceeding for the same offense was pending in the United States remains unclear. DeWolf might have hired Manchester to report the crime and rewarded him later with employment on DeWolf vessels, or if Manchester had arrived in Statia of his own accord, DeWolf might have bought the man's silence with future employment if he would stop pursuing him. Despite the unknowns, the fact remains that specific witnesses were summoned and likely coached by DeWolf, in hopes that with his exoneration he could return to the United States a free man. It appeared that as a result of Statia's status as a major slave depot at that time, DeWolf believed there would be less legal opposition regarding the death of a slave if he were put on trial for murder. He was correct in this risky assumption.

Not surprisingly, Manchester, who reported DeWolf's crime in the West Indies, began a financially lucrative relationship with DeWolf and his brothers. Shortly after the trial and less than one year later, on September 15, 1795, Manchester left on his first slaving voyage as a DeWolf captain.

In June 1796, he successfully delivered 149 slaves for his new employer to Savannah, Georgia. Manchester completed at least five more voyages for DeWolf and his brothers by 1806. Additionally, Manchester became a sole financial backer of one slaving voyage and a co-investor with Charles Collins, DeWolf's brother-in-law, on another voyage, both in 1799.[83] Before his involvement in the trial in St. Thomas, Manchester was just another Rhode Island captain for hire. Upon his return home, he surprisingly became a financial success with DeWolf's help. Both Manchester and Collins shared in liberal profits from slaving under the mentorship of DeWolf.

Back in Rhode Island, DeWolf's family worked tirelessly behind the scenes to ensure the dismissal of the charges against DeWolf in Rhode Island.[84] Their immense power would have created opportunities for undue influence within the community as well. Undoubtedly, this would have included James's father-in-law, Senator Bradford. Although there were two different courts in two separate countries addressing the same charges for murder, there was value in an exoneration verdict in either location. With the murder case regarding the *Polly* dropped in St. Thomas, all that DeWolf needed to do was to wait for the Federal Grand Jury of Rhode Island to repeal the warrant for his arrest. This is where DeWolf's family and extended family asserted tremendous influence. Certainly, Senator Bradford did his part to influence the warrant's nullification in support of his daughter and son-in-law. Additionally, Rhode Island marshal William Peck declared that he could never find DeWolf, who was a very prominent member of an eminent and highly visible family, in order to arrest him. After purportedly searching for multiple years, Peck declared that he would finally stop looking.[85]

In 1795, Judge Henry Marchant reviewed DeWolf's case, reportedly at the request of his family and perhaps Senator Bradford, who were also in possession of the second deposition. Marchant was Rhode Island's first federally appointed judge, placed into this esteemed position by President Washington, and the one person who stood between DeWolf and his freedom.[86] A combination of factors that were clearly in DeWolf's favor could have influenced the judge to arrange for the warrant's expiration. DeWolf's father-in-law, who owned two slaves, was a powerful and influential member in politics. He had personally attempted to assist DeWolf three years earlier by independently delivering a letter to Judge Jay from DeWolf requesting leniency in regards to the charges of murder. The second factor that helped sway Marchant's decision was the reality that he, too, owned a slave and perhaps did not feel the urgency to see someone charged and convicted of murdering a slave.[87] Ultimately, the DeWolf family was able to send word to James with the message that although the charges for murder had not officially been dropped, the arrest warrant had, making it safe for him to return home from the West Indies.[88] DeWolf returned immediately to his empire and his determined nemesis, Ellery.

Chapter 3

LAWS AND ECONOMICS

*A most colorful and historic figure, James became the most successful member of
the DeWolf clan, dominating the seaport town of Bristol for years.*

During the time the colonies were fighting for independence from Britain
by boycotting British goods, the tiny state of Rhode Island turned
a blind eye. Newport had an unusually strong Tory faction that staunchly
supported the king of England. These men were motivated to make money,
and the colony became known as a haven for merchant captains who could
be assured that they could illegally land their cargo. Even under the guise of
the British Crown, Rhode Island had the reputation for being a rebellious
colony with a blatant disregard for the law. Rhode Island had developed a
precedent of defying the king; it would also challenge the new Constitution
developed by our forefathers and continue to ignore the laws written by
both local and federal governments. It became only natural for the seafaring
state to make the transition from ignoring the law regarding boycotts to
transferring its energy to the illegal trafficking of humans. Rhode Island
continued to be known as a state filled with Tories, in support of the Crown,
which bolstered defiance for most laws. Despite these encumbrances, William
Ellery continued to build his reputation as a politician and a Patriot.[89]

At the onset of 1784, the American Revolution had just ended, the first
U.S. ship to trade with China set sail from New York and John Jay became
our first secretary of state of foreign affairs. It was also when Rhode Island's
Gradual Emancipation Act of 1784 was introduced, just as DeWolf's success

began to grow.[90] Unsurprisingly, slavers, including DeWolf, opposed the act, fighting hard to block its passage. The law outlined that all children born to slaves after March 1, 1784, were to be free; slaves between the ages of fifteen and twenty-five would become indentured servants and be freed after seven years; and slaves twenty-five and older would remain slaves for life.[91] Heavily supported by a large contingent of Rhode Island Quakers and abolitionists, it was considered one of the most significant Revolution-inspired statutes ever written, yet it was readily ignored.[92]

Strong efforts were made to secure immediate freedom for slaves and to influence the complacent attitude toward slavery in general. Abolitionists expected state prosecutors, customs officials and even private citizens to report those who broke this new law. Although the law addressed the issue of abolishing domestic slavery, Rhode Island slaveholders were slow to respond, delaying emancipation in their state.[93] Many Rhode Islanders either refused or neglected to report violations of the law because their financial prosperity depended on the success of the illegal trade. Therefore, the law had little impact on the slave trade in Rhode Island.[94] Though the law might have been written to outlaw slavery, what was even more significant was that it neglected to outlaw slave merchants.[95]

In 1787, the State of Rhode Island addressed the issue of slavery once again and passed a revision to the 1784 law. In addition to its original statutes, the revised law finally addressed slave merchants and imposed a fine on any shipowner who imported slaves into the state.[96] This particular law set a penalty of $100 for every slave transported and $1,000 for every vessel so engaged and explicitly forbade the importation of slaves into Rhode Island.[97] Nonetheless, the revised law still did not address the topic of slave merchants' involvement in the slave trade outside Rhode Island, leaving a liberally interpreted loophole.

Realizing the state neglected to enforce the Act of 1787, DeWolf blatantly sailed undetected down discrete water passages throughout Narragansett Bay until he reached his destination of Bristol. Rhode Island abolitionists continued to protest this and the activity of other local slavers, only to discover that their leaders refused to respond. The motivation to allow illegal slaving to continue both domestically and internationally was based, in part, on the fact that the slave trade was the backbone of Rhode Island's economy.[98] It wasn't until much later that Rhode Island slave traders ceased their illegal activity locally, isolating their involvement to the southern states and internationally. Continuing in this lucrative business overshadowed the reality of its illegal and immoral nature.

Initially, Rhode Island's economic foundation was built on fishing, trading and shipbuilding, yet its numerous seaports and expansive access to the Atlantic Ocean encouraged the emergence of the slave trade.[99] But once the profits from slaving began to grow in the middle of the eighteenth century, an increase in local commerce occurred in Rhode Island. In response to the strengthening economic climate, a large number of residents became employed at rum distilleries, and a growing number of bankers, creditors and insurance agents began to emerge to support the rapidly growing shipbuilding and slaving industry.[100]

Many of these enterprising businesses were established by DeWolf, who took advantage of the positive economic climate in Bristol and became a successful businessman. DeWolf had the tenacious ability and savvy business sense to take his family to a level of financial prosperity that far exceeded that of many successful families in Rhode Island. Initially, the entire DeWolf legacy was built solely on his connection with the slave trade. Near the end of his empire, there were local textile mills and sugar and coffee plantations in Cuba that added to the abundant DeWolf estate.

Although DeWolf had a keen sense for slave trading, it was his uncle, Simeon Potter, who became a mentor and continually advised DeWolf on alternative sailing routes to avoid prosecution and to protect his dominant position, not only in the trade, but in the community as well. Included were explicit directions and explanations on how to circumvent slave laws in high-risk areas. Letters with advice from Potter allowed DeWolf and his brothers to make at least 103 known slaving voyages along the famed transatlantic triangular trade route up until December 31, 1807.[101] This number of voyages tremendously exceeded the participation by any other individual or family from the United States. However, DeWolf and his family orchestrated many more slaving voyages than have been previously documented before, and well beyond, the year 1808.

The unique design of the triangle trade enabled slaving vessels to maximize their efficiency by making one huge import and export loop. When a vessel departed from the coast of Africa, it faced a treacherous section of travel referred to as the Middle Passage. Once a captain began his travel through the Middle Passage, the concern was simply to get his human cargo safely to market.[102]

For the slaves, the nightmare first began when they witnessed the immensity of the ocean, since many had been kidnapped inland with no previous exposure to such expansive water. Slave traders would at times try to capture or, more commonly, purchase their entire cargo of slaves in one

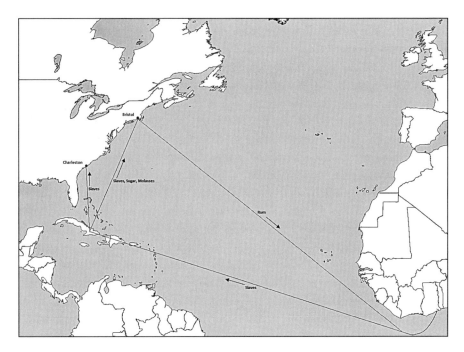

DeWolf's transatlantic triangle trade route map. DeWolf's routes remained unique in that he had financial control at each destination through his vertically integrated empire. *Map created for the author by Tim Clinton.*

or perhaps two ports in Africa as quickly as possible. This would not only reduce expenses but also would decrease the chance of mortality among the human cargo once the journey began. If two ports were used, it was necessary for the captain to keep the first group of slaves on board, with an increased risk of health issues such as smallpox or dysentery. This small change in the voyage would escalate the possibility for death among the slave population and overall financial loss for the captain. As the slaves were forced on board, their fears turned to the length of the journey, the open sea and where the vessel was taking them.[103]

It was common for slaves to be stowed in the lower hold of the ship lying on their backs or sides, wedged together like spoons. Another common practice was to have many people chained together, or chained to the floor, to limit movement in order to diminish the possibility of an uprising.[104] The lower hold was a suffocating, dark space, overcrowded with the stench of disease, human waste and rot that only grew stronger as the weeks-long journey progressed. There were times when the slaves, in controlled settings, were allowed on deck for the purpose of breathing fresh air—not because of an underlying sense of compassion but to aid in maintaining good health, ensuring their captors' financial profit. But when there was stormy weather and the seas dangerously tossed the vessel, the slaves were forced to stay below deck. Slaves were most likely huddled in terror, particularly when the hatch to the lower hold was locked when there was fear of a revolt. There was torture, brutal beatings and rape of the slaves, with the perpetual presence of both disease and death. The Middle Passage was the most treacherous part of the journey for the slaves, amassing an average 15 percent mortality rate that could actually reduce the overall profits of a sale by as much as 30 percent.[105]

Not only was the Middle Passage horrible for slaves, but captains and crew would suffer as well. If a voyage ran long as a result of unreliable trade winds, food and water would, at times, run out. Incidences of insurrections and mutinies were known to happen, and with the threat of infectious disease, staggering losses for both the cargo and crew occurred. Maritime logs in Rhode Island recorded a number of tragedies involving slaving vessels, including ships that were struck by lightning, which killed the entire crew, and ships that mysteriously disappeared without a trace.[106] The varieties of wretchedness that a crew endured on the Middle Passage made it one of the least desirable sailing assignments. Yet captains and crew members, such as the DeWolfs and those in their employ, would greedily continue to sail on slaving voyages time and time again, as the majority of voyages proved to be financially lucrative.

The length of the Middle Passage was determined by the time of year the vessel set sail from the African coast and the direction the trade winds blew. The trade winds made it difficult to get away from the African coast for most of the year, but once the ship reached the open sea, the winds typically pushed the vessel along.[107] If the ship was sailing leeward, the trip from Africa was of extended length, as the vessel had to fight the ocean's currents. This forced the captain to sail a circuitous return route until he could pick up the northeasterly trade winds. This leg of the journey could last eight to ten weeks and sometimes longer. With this, the vessel became subjected to extended equatorial heat and sudden storms, requiring closure of the holds and furthering the already unbearable conditions for the slaves.[108] Frequently, this weather pattern required the vessel to make a stop in the West Indies, if for no other reason than to replenish supplies. As a result of the prolonged trips during leeward trades, captains often made quick sales of some of their slaves in the West Indies before the cargo became seriously ill or died during the last leg of the journey to Cuba or the United States.[109]

However, if the vessel sailed windward, away from Africa, it sailed with the southeasterly trade winds, allowing a much shorter travel time through the Middle Passage. This allowed a vessel to choose to bypass the West Indies and sail directly to Cuba or the United States, shortening the trip and increasing the survival rate and health of the slaves. Despite the variation in trade winds and the risks involved in sailing the last leg of a journey from Africa during a windward voyage, the ultimate determining factor of the final destination was dictated by the prices in the individual slave markets.[110]

There were a variety of ports throughout the Atlantic that involved transporting products for trade—most importantly rum—from the United States to Africa. Once the vessels arrived at the African coast, the products were traded for slaves, also referred to as black cargo or just plain cargo. From there, the route often continued on to the West Indies or Cuba, where several Americans and Europeans owned sugar and coffee plantations. Here, some of the slaves and other goods were offloaded and traded for sugar. The route typically carried the ship back to its original port, loaded with the most important and financially valuable product: sugar and raw sugar cane.

Once it arrived to the homeport, the sugar cane juice would be processed into molasses for the purpose of distilling it into rum to later be traded for slaves. The process repeated itself time and time again. Clearly, modifications sometimes were made to the routes, but the outcome remained the same: the illegal trafficking of humans. James DeWolf had a clear vision for how each point of the triangle trade could benefit him personally, establishing a vertically integrated empire with business enterprises at each port.

In Bristol, DeWolf owned distilleries that employed local residents and each day turned an average of 300 gallons of molasses into 250 gallons of rum.[111] This was stored in barrels, called hogsheads, which usually held 63 gallons of rum each. Commonly, a local cooper would be contracted to build hogsheads for the distilleries. A receipt signed by DeWolf's brother John showed that the average cost was $1.50 for one barrel.[112] There was a thriving business for the construction of hogsheads in the town of Bristol. DeWolf then loaded the rum, along with other miscellaneous and less profitable items for sale or trade, onto his vessels and sailed for the western coast of Africa.

DeWolf's mission included not only the acquisition of slaves for himself but also the fulfillment of purchase requests from both northerners and southerners. These transactions were done either directly or through their agents. Once DeWolf's vessels arrived in Africa, primarily on the Gold Coast, the rum and other items were sold or traded for slaves. It is believed that

Excavation findings of rum casks that were once part of a rum distillery in Bristol. *Photo courtesy of Dr. Matthew C. Perry, private collection.*

DeWolf worked consistently with specific agents in Africa that he personally employed, but no concrete evidence can substantiate this notion.

The two most frequented stops made along the African coast by the DeWolfs were the present-day Gulf of Guinea in Ghana and slightly northwest in the Guinea-Bissau region. Letters written by the DeWolf brothers would frequently state specific geographical ports of orientation on the coast of Africa. In one such letter, John DeWolf wrote to his brother Levi from Annamaboe, a centrally located region of Ghana, and another letter that James wrote to Levi was sent from Christiansborg, located on the Gold Coast.[113]

After completing final transactions on the African coast, DeWolf would set sail for the West Indies and then the United States. After 1808, he stopped frequently in the bays of Havana or Matanzas, Cuba, where he owned coffee and sugar plantations. In the nineteenth century, plantations in the region of Cuba were referred to as estates and were cultivated by hundreds of slaves. During the harvest season on these plantations, slaves worked sixteen to twenty intensely demanding hours each day. As a result of this agonizing workload in a brutal climate, many slaves survived only eight to ten years, resulting in an unusually high mortality rate. It was not uncommon for plantation owners to periodically replace an entire population of slaves in Cuba.[114]

DeWolf dropped off slaves, often replenishing his own estates, and picked up more sugar from his plantations. Once the vessel was reloaded with the remaining slaves and hogsheads, the slaves would be delivered to market in the South. On the final leg of the journey, DeWolf sailed back to Bristol and delivered multiple barrels of sugar to his own distilleries. Most of the rum distilleries were in the North, with many located in Rhode Island. Ironically, DeWolf's father-in-law, U.S. senator William Bradford, owned Bristol's largest rum distillery with the knowledge that the rum he produced was being traded for slaves and supported his son-in-law in this illegal activity.[115] Once DeWolf's ships were reloaded, the process of the triangle trade route started again, repeating the same pattern and giving DeWolf complete control over his profit margins. Monitoring supply and demand, DeWolf determined the best time to buy and sell specific merchandise, particularly slaves, both domestically and internationally.

In 1800, Congress passed a revision to the act of 1794, adding a vital amendment to the law. The revision clarified that it was prohibited to transport slaves from the United States to *any* foreign country, even if slavery was legal in that specific jurisdiction; outfit a ship for the purposes of importing slaves; or be employed in the slave trade. A two-year prison term had been added, along with an additional $100 fine per crew member. This was specifically designed to target American citizens who continued to serve voluntarily on slave vessels and act as slave traders, such as the DeWolf clan.[116]

Continuing with the development of his empire, James and his brother William founded the Bank of Bristol in 1797 to safeguard the family's money. Two generations of DeWolfs became chief stockholders.[117] Housed in an elegant three-story brick, Georgian-style structure, which maintains its original appearance today, the bank also served as the counting house or accounting department for James's and William's other enterprises, all of which were involved in the slave trade in some capacity. The DeWolfs conveniently built the structure at the port of Bristol in Narragansett Bay. The bank was situated on a piece of property owned by William, who in turn leased the land to the Bank of Bristol for $150 per year.[118]

In 1800, the Bank of Bristol was officially chartered with $50,000 in capital ($700,000 in twenty-first-century dollars) creating Bristol's first bank.[119] The DeWolfs appointed as their first president James's father-in-law. He was followed later by John DeWolf. This scenario allowed James endless possibilities to continue to assert total financial domination over the town and his family. Initially, the establishment of small local banks was to accept deposits and charge interest on loans. It did not take long for those

Bank of Bristol, built by James DeWolf and his brother, photo circa 1900. The building remained nearly unchanged one century later. *Photo courtesy of Mary Millard, private collection.*

banks to begin providing other services, such as issuing banknotes (checks), exchanging heavy coins for paper money and exchanging currencies from other countries. DeWolf's counting room was originally located on the ground floor of the bank, and allegedly, the basement held slaves in a

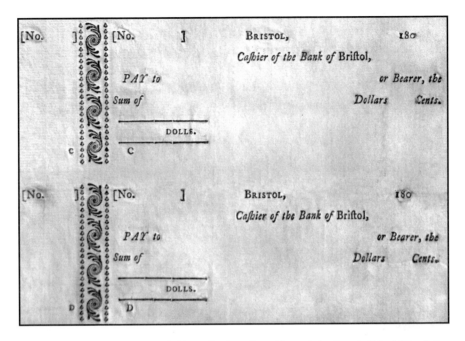

Checks from the Bank of Bristol. *Photo taken by author, with permission from the Bristol Historical and Preservation Society.*

A one-dollar note from the Bank of Mount Hope, signed by DeWolf, president, and brother-in-law Bryon Diman, cashier. A piece was cut out when pulled from circulation. *Photo taken by author, with permission from the Bristol Historical and Preservation Society.*

dungeon-like atmosphere. Interestingly, DeWolf shortly thereafter started a second bank, just two buildings north, named Mount Hope Bank. James was listed as the first president of this financial establishment.[120]

There were no banking regulations imposed by the federal government at the time the Bank of Bristol received its charter. This gave independent banks the freedom to choose the location for the bank's structure and to pay whatever interest was required to obtain funds. They also judged and acquired assets yielding the highest return.[121] The DeWolfs maintained voting authority over the financial decisions made for their bank, which implies that the DeWolf family owned at least 51 percent of the stock, if not the entire institution. Residents of Bristol, including the DeWolfs, would deposit their monies into the Bank of Bristol, establishing revenue for the institution's loans. This further empowered the DeWolfs, allowing them

Diman Counting House, owned by the DeWolfs and attached to their warehouse, circa 1900. *Photo courtesy of Mary Millard, private collection.*

flexibility in determining interest rates and fees. They maintained control over who received loans, including their family members, allowing the DeWolfs to make loans to themselves interest free, if they chose, using their depositors' money to support their thriving business in the slave trade.

As the Bank of Bristol became more successful, it was necessary for the DeWolfs to build a new counting house directly next door and on the water's edge at Bristol Harbor. This separated the bank and the accounting portion of DeWolf's enterprises. The DeWolfs then added on a warehouse to the counting house. It included a boat slip that ran alongside the building, enabling the DeWolfs' vessels to easily dock to load and unload their cargo.

The warehouse and counting house were located in one long, narrow building with two stories above ground, a basement that still maintains restraint shackles attached to the walls and a gabled roof. The entire structure was built from red and gray granite collected in Africa and the West Indies. The granite was brought back to Bristol in DeWolf's vessels as ballast, helping to weigh down and stabilize his ships while traveling along the trade route, particularly the Middle Passage. It was common practice for captains to put stones in the hulls of their vessels to stabilize their ships through rough and stormy waters.[122]

DeWolf Wharf Estates (2013), which included the Bank of Bristol (left), the Diman Counting House (right) and the granite warehouse. The staircases were added in the last century. *Photo taken by author.*

A close up of the granite used as ballast and then to build the DeWolf warehouse; large slabs were utilized to create openings for windows and doors. *Photo taken by author.*

DeWolf's ability to maximize his efficiency on some voyages by using granite instead of stones to replace the rum was a brilliant idea and aided to the stabilization of the voyage from Africa. However, it would have taken years to accumulate enough granite to construct a large building. The exterior walls of each room remained in their natural state of exposed granite. The windows, strategically placed throughout both floors, allowed in natural sunlight, and the window and doors were framed with massive, individual pieces of granite. The granite building still stands today, with minor upgrades, modernizing the facility for present-day use as a restaurant and tavern.

Some have challenged that using granite as ballast to replace rum was not logical, as the human cargo being transported back to America would make up the difference in weight. However, when multiple possibilities and scenarios were calculated, the human cargo would not equal the weight of hogsheads of rum once they were left on the coast of Africa. For example, in general terms, allowing for slight variations in weight, the following is a simple breakdown of what a variety of cargo would weigh:

1 hogshead = 63 American gallons, approximately
1 hogshead of water = 526 pounds, approximately
1 hogshead of rum = 449 pounds, approximately
1 hogshead of molasses = 712 pounds, approximately
1 adult African male in 1800 = on average 155 pounds[123]

If you carried ten hogsheads of fresh water and twenty hogsheads of rum to the coast of Africa, this cargo alone would weigh approximately 14,231 pounds. Then you must include additional items for trade, as well as food that were also stored in hogsheads and would increase the overall weight for cargo on board. Carrying back to America half the fresh water plus one hundred adult males would average 18,130 pounds. However, DeWolf never returned with a load of exclusively adult males. DeWolf's cargo manifests always included women, children and infants at a much lower weight ratio overall. In most cases, women, children and infants outnumbered the total amount of adult males on board. As a result, it was possible to return to Bristol each time with a small load of granite as additional ballast, weighing as little as 2,000 pounds.[124] With the number of vessels in DeWolf's fleet and the numerous trips to Africa that he personally orchestrated each year, eventually enough granite was collected to build this architectural accomplishment.

It can be suggested that it was unnecessary to carry granite to Bristol from Africa and the West Indies when there was granite quarried in Maine, New Hampshire and Massachusetts. However, at the time of DeWolf's construction in Bristol, the quarry in Maine was not operating. (It opened in 1820.) The Fall River, Massachusetts quarry, which would have been the most logical location, did not open until 1840, three years after DeWolf's death. Finally, the first granite business documented in New Hampshire was not even established until 1883.[125] Black, gray and red granite, along with many other colors, were commonly found in many areas of Africa and throughout the Caribbean.[126]

The DeWolf wharves, often referred to as the "Wharf Estates" by DeWolf, provided facilities for crew members of outgoing slavers and were located on Thames Street, the location of many of his other businesses. DeWolf's distillery was located here, and it cost approximately ten cents a gallon for the distillation process. DeWolf also paid five cents per gallon duty for the molasses but received a three-cent rebate from the federal government, called drawback, when he exported the rum. This is clearly a conflict of interest that was created by the federal government, as the business of slave trading was illegal, but the exportation of locally distilled rum was financially rewarded. The distillery alone was successful enough for DeWolf to accumulate adequate wealth to sustain him for the rest of his life.[127] In addition to the distillery, warehouses and wharves, the DeWolfs owned many retail stores throughout Bristol.[128]

Facing pressure from the revised laws, DeWolf continued to add to the success of his business enterprises by opening a local insurance company.

Joining with his brothers and naming his new business venture after his estate, DeWolf established the Mount Hope Insurance Company and served as president.[129] It functioned with a double purpose: making available the government-mandated insurance coverage to local mariners and insuring DeWolf slave ships and cargo going in and out of the port of Bristol.[130] Insurance policies covered all vessels, including those that participated in the slave trade, against damage or total destruction from shipwreck, loss of the ship or cargo to piracy, confiscation at a foreign port or disease that killed a certain predetermined percentage of slaves.[131] The political environment, maritime slaving laws, war or threat of war contributed to the total cost and value of insurance policies.[132] Once the threat level was determined, the percentage of cargo lost was estimated. This could range from a 5 to 25 percent replacement of cargo before a payment would be issued. The amount of the overall coverage would then be established, a contract written and signed and the premium paid in full.

One insurance policy for a DeWolf vessel in 1801 established that the "cargo" was to be insured at a 15 percent loss, with the premium established at $600.[133] However, sound business practice seemed to negate the logic of insuring one's own vessels. By today's legal standards, it could be construed as insurance fraud. If the cargo were lost, the DeWolfs risked bankruptcy or extensive payouts that could create a tremendous amount of personal debt both to the insurer and the insured. Fortunately for James DeWolf, he never lost a vessel or a substantial amount of cargo. At the family's height of financial power, the DeWolfs predictably made considerable profits from the sale of policies to other shipowners that covered the vessels if a catastrophic event occurred.[134] Additionally, it is likely that the purchase of insurance for their vessels existed on paper only. This potentially generated additional income as an insurance company while allowing the DeWolfs to cover their own vessels, according to law, at no cost to them.

As a highly successful slave trader, James DeWolf owned all of his vessels outright. DeWolf also held 75 percent interest in many other vessels, primarily those owned by his brothers and extended relatives.[135] Levi, John and William, in addition to James, also owned shares in numerous local American slavers.[136]

All of these business ventures provided consistent income for DeWolf and his family, along with employment for many in the community. Seemingly, DeWolf had achieved success in every aspect of the slave trade with the exception of one final detail: his ability to bypass William Ellery, the customhouse collector for Rhode Island who was also an ardent abolitionist.

Chapter 4

THE PIOUS BROTHER

Levi quit the trade in disgust after a single voyage, and spent the rest of his life with his Bible.
—*DeWolf family lore*

Many historians, relying heavily on family lore, recount that Levi, the youngest son of Mark Anthony DeWolf, sailed on his maiden voyage in 1791 at the age of twenty-five.[137] Once he returned to Bristol from this voyage, family descendants believe that Levi quit the slave trade and the family business, which were so cleverly intertwined. In reality, for generations, the DeWolfs had been quoted as referring to Levi as "Quakerish"; he was the family member, along with his sisters, who brought piety to the slave traders.[138] Levi was baptized in the Congregational Church of Bristol on October 26, 1766, at the age of six months, negating the possibility that he was an active Quaker. However, he clearly demonstrated more religious fervor than the other DeWolf men, particularly his brother and business partner James.

During Levi's lifetime, Quaker meetings were not held within the town of Bristol. The nearest town that conducted Quaker services, Portsmouth, would have taken hours to reach by horse or wagon.[139] However, generations of DeWolfs have declared that Levi was known to sit in solitude reading his Bible and other religious books, a trait that might have seemed Quakerish to the family and community. Levi was known to be a loyal husband and devoted father, which can clearly be seen in his letters to his wife, Lydia, while on his many voyages. Furthermore,

Levi DeWolf tended to his onion farm when he was home from voyages. He was born on April 8, 1766, and died on July 18, 1848. He married Lydia Smith on August 19, 1792. *Reverend Calbraith Perry, DeWolf Genealogy, 1902, with permission and rights owned by the Bristol Historical and Preservation Society.*

Lydia seemingly was the most religiously devout of the DeWolf wives, according to church records, which would undoubtedly have influenced her husband's belief system. Levi encouraged his children to continue with their religious devotion throughout their lives as he and his wife continued to attend the Congregational Church of Bristol.[140] Despite Levi's commitment to the church, he sailed on his first voyage in 1791 and continued to sail for his brother James until as late as 1806, if not later. It was unquestionably vital for Levi to fill in for his brother James during his four years of exile in the West Indies. Levi assumed a major part of James's role in the family business regardless of the local belief that he had quit the trade. However, the question remains whether Levi continued to participate willingly or felt pressure from his brother to continue in the family business.[141]

Occasionally, DeWolf told Levi to make his way to either the West Indies or Cuba specifically so that the two could spend some time together. This was particularly true when DeWolf was sequestered in the West Indies from 1791 to 1795 while avoiding arrest in Rhode Island. There are additional ledgers that outline the balance sheet activities at the end of each voyage and letters with full reports of each voyage sent from Levi to DeWolf. Much of this correspondence discussed which voyage Levi would go on next and in which vessel, the investors and their personal slave requests and what cargo Levi would pick up in Africa and deliver to either Havana or Matanzas, Cuba.[142] Interestingly, Levi's assistance to his brother and sustained involvement in the slave trade during the time DeWolf was sequestered in the West Indies unveils the reality. James could not have succeeded so easily in Statia if not for the help and expertise of Levi. Volumes of correspondence between James and his brother confirmed Levi's prolonged involvement in the trade, not only during DeWolf's four-year hiatus, but afterward as well.

For years, historians recounted the original tale of Levi's objections to being involved in the trade. This, in part, was due to a family memoir written by George Howe, a distant DeWolf relative. In his writings, Howe speaks of Levi on ten separate occasions. Influencing the reader to believe that Levi lived a life of piety, Howe began by describing Levi's devotion to reading his Bible. Levi was also referred to as Quakerish or pious on five separate occasions within Howe's book, *Mount Hope*. In the remaining references, Levi was referred to as a poor farmer with a modest home who was outside the more elite circle in Bristol. Levi's home was in fact more humble than that of his brother James, and he did maintain a small farm. However, it is easy to understand how a reader could misinterpret Howe's version of Levi's distaste for the trade and rely so heavily on folklore. The opinion of the reader unquestionably shifted away from the stark reality of Levi's involvement in the slave trade and was retold incorrectly for generations.[143]

James relied heavily on Levi for many years, which resulted in an investment of time, teaching him specific strategies to circumvent the slave trade laws as they became stricter. Levi, seemingly, was a willing participant. On October 24, 1794, James wrote to Levi regarding how things were becoming difficult in the port of Bristol as a result of the Act of 1794. Congress had passed this act, further prohibiting the transport of slaves from the United States to any foreign country, as well as making it illegal for American citizens to outfit a ship for purposes of importing slaves or to be employed in the slave trade. Knowing that they were involved in illegal activity, James told Levi that he needed to underwrite his ships and cargo for a higher value than usual and encouraged him to try to find a second underwriter to do the same. By twice insuring a particular vessel during a legally risky time, the second policy would help to safeguard DeWolf's investment from significant loss while guaranteeing replacement of his personal property if their vessel were seized by the federal government or lost at sea. James then directed Levi that the insurance policy should cover his vessel, granting them the ability to touch any port in the Union, including Rhode Island, to drop off slaves without fear or risk of seizure or financial loss.[144]

Once DeWolf was able to return home to Bristol in 1795, Levi continued to be directed by his brother in future slaving ventures. In a letter written in

1797, this time from Levi to James, Levi explained that the Havana slave market was thriving with inflated prices and that the slavers from Rhode Island had exceedingly benefitted.[145] Communication between the DeWolf brothers was extensive but, at the same time, imperative to maintain such a lucrative business. Levi was sole or part owner of at least eight independent voyages beginning in 1790 and ending in 1800.[146] Levi not only helped James while he resided in the West Indies, but he also remained involved in slaving for, at the very minimum, six additional years after DeWolf returned home. DeWolf's shipping ledgers would imply his involvement for even longer, as "Captain Levi DeWolf" can be seen written on several pages in DeWolf's shipping ledgers well past 1810. However, there is no evidence after the Act of 1808 that Levi was a willing participant in the transportation of slaves on his voyages.[147]

In the correspondence between the two brothers, there is a letter dated December 16, 1791, that reports to James of Levi's bartering for some slaves from a Portuguese boat. The ship records from this voyage showed that Levi sold 109 slaves for $28,200. In this shipment, there was the death of one male and one female slave, which was considered a low percentage of loss for slaving voyages. Also found in letters from James to Levi are instructions on revised tactics to avoid trouble with the law in both domestic and international waters.[148]

On August 9, 1793, Levi was in Statia with a cargo of slaves while James was still living in the West Indies. Levi wrote a letter to his wife telling her that he was safe, as he had been gone nearly six months without the possibility of sending a word. He also informed her that he would sail to St. Croix the next day to meet James, who stated that once Levi arrived he would help him sell his cargo.[149]

By the end of the same month, James wrote to Levi and cautioned him about the procedure of presenting slaves as a port requirement to the collector in Cuba in order to purchase sugar. The letter is succinct and quite businesslike. It is instructional and included useful advice for Levi as he represented James in this transfer of cargo. DeWolf became quite specific; he outlined the names of the collector and the agent with whom Levi was to do business. He stated in detail the custom for entrance and that he must first apply for a permit and then to go to the collector and get permission to transfer the sugar to the customhouse. DeWolf finalized his instructions by telling Levi to go to the collector to request the items that DeWolf had previously stored at the customhouse. At the end of the letter, below DeWolf's signature in a postscript, he informed Levi that he would arrive

Levi DeWolf correspondence where he mentioned that James's family was in the West Indies and that they would join Levi on his trip to St. Thomas. *Provided by Mary Millard, private collection.*

the following morning to meet him, demonstrating his mobility even though he was in hiding.[150] DeWolf had already established a financially lucrative relationship for trade in Havana.

The following day, September 1, 1793, Levi wrote to his wife again. He told her of his frustration at his continued struggle to sell his cargo and that he had yet to leave for Cuba. He stated that James was able to sell about half of the cargo but that he now needed to sail to Havana to sell the rest. Three days later, on the fourth, Levi was still in St. Croix and wrote yet again to his wife, seemingly annoyed at the endless delays. In this letter, he told Lydia that he would be leaving for St. Thomas and then hopefully Havana in the next couple of days. He closed by stating that he would be meeting not only James but also his brother's family, who were sailing with James to Cuba.[151]

Many descendants have questioned the theory that DeWolf stayed in Statia while evading arrest from 1791 until 1795, as he fathered two children with his wife, who presumably never saw James during this time period. As evidenced by his many letters, DeWolf did not stay in one place during his four-year exile but instead moved about quite freely, using Statia as his staging port. With the vast collection of ships in DeWolf's possession, it does not seem unreasonable for his family to have sailed frequently to the Caribbean on holiday adventures, as evidenced in the letter Levi wrote to his wife on September 4, 1793. Additionally, DeWolf wrote numerous letters in which he mentioned his family visiting him in the West Indies.

After many years of successful voyages, DeWolf confidently sent Levi on an important trip to Havana in January 1800 with the intent of handling a substantial amount of business, including the collection of money owed. The letter is written in extraordinary detail and conveys just how much activity DeWolf was involved in regarding the trade and the fleet of vessels he owned. It also confirmed, once again, Levi's continued involvement in the family business. First, DeWolf sent Levi to Havana in a chartered sloop called the *Ranger*. It is an unusual account for DeWolf to have had chartered a vessel when he owned so many, but the letter goes on to explain that at the moment, all of DeWolf's vessels were in transport. Levi's assignment was to deliver a letter to David Nagle, as he was at that time in charge of all DeWolf's business in Havana. This was followed by a discussion of the DeWolf schooner *Chances*, as it had experienced a time-consuming and financially debilitating shipwreck on a Cuban reef. Levi was to speak with the captain of that schooner about the cargo, as all of the slaves had been rescued and sold. This news was followed by instructions on how to resolve the situation of the disabled vessel. Within the deeply instructional letter, he mentioned that the captain was able to commandeer the lame vessel enough to successfully sell part of his cargo in Havana for $800 and was able to make his way to Matanzas to sell his remaining cargo of slaves for $4,800 before the ship became entirely paralyzed.[152]

DeWolf continued his correspondence by stating to Levi that if his brig *Stork* was in port in Havana, he should do everything in his power to dispatch it for home immediately with $10,000 from the sale of slaves and also outlined a list of what was to be shipped as cargo. DeWolf vessels that sailed directly from Cuba to Rhode Island primarily carried sugar from his plantations Mount Hope or Nueva Esperanza (New Hope).[153] He concluded the financial aspect of the instructions by directing Levi to take the profits and give $8,000 each to two different DeWolf captains to bring home on their independent voyages, paying each captain $10 for this additional responsibility. DeWolf expanded his instructions by stating that there was a gentleman in Havana from whom Levi needed to collect money, that he should sail home with a vessel filled with sugar or molasses and that he should personally carry the remaining profits.[154] It becomes quite clear that DeWolf's dependence on Levi was paramount to his continued success.

Finally, DeWolf gave further course of action, stating that if his schooner *Juno* was in port when Levi arrived in Havana, Levi was to direct the captain

Watercolor of the Nueva Esperanza (New Hope) estate in Cuba, presumed to be painted by George Howe, discovered in his personal diary, dated 1832–34. *Photo taken by author, with permission and rights owned by the Bristol Historical and Preservation Society.*

to sail it to St. Thomas to be painted or sold and that the vessel *Sally* was to be sold as is. Within this one letter, DeWolf discussed with Levi seven separate DeWolf vessels and the action that was to be taken with each one. He then further contemplated the financial aspects of Levi's responsibilities specific to carrying home $46,000 in cash. DeWolf brilliantly decided to have Levi divide the money into equal parts among the separate captains, with the remaining and largest amount of $30,000 for Levi to personally handle. This would ultimately ensure the safe arrival of the money and demonstrated DeWolf's entrepreneurial giftedness and accumulating wealth but also, and more importantly, his reliance on his brothers.[155]

Levi's involvement in the family business did not stop when he was not personally on a slaving vessel. He would garner information for his brother from various contacts he personally maintained in varying ports. This can be noted in a letter Levi received from a man for whom he was trying to help find employment while in Havana. Within this correspondence, there was the report to Levi that slaves were being sold at that time for $450 to $500 each. The man also included the current market prices in Havana regarding white sugar, brown sugar and molasses, all of which would be information Levi passed on to James.[156]

Many will question, once again, Levi's true involvement in the slave trade as a result of nonspecifics listed in much of his correspondence to his family. Levi wrote to his wife while on board a slave vessel on February 11, 1806. Typically, the originator of the letter would include the city where it was written, but in this instance, Levi wrote the date and, right below it, that he was writing while at sea on the *Semiramis*. Because he could not state the city he was presently in, Levi instead listed the latitude, 27.48N, and longitude, 72.11W. This particular location is east of Florida and northeast of Cuba. He spoke of the treacherous passage that he had encountered and successfully navigated his way through, with relief, while on his way to Cuba, at the same time musing that he missed Lydia and the children.[157]

There is only one reason for Levi to have purposely sailed through the Middle Passage: the acquisition of slaves. Maintaining consistent discretion in all correspondence by the DeWolfs and their captains, slaves were often referred to as cargo, but in this case, Levi referred to his cargo as "Articles," even going so far as to capitalize the word. While on this same voyage, Levi wrote a second letter, this time to James, from Havana on February 20, 1806. In it, Levi was quite specific about his voyage and sailing on DeWolf's vessel the *Semiramis*. He stated that it was an exceptional ship that sailed remarkably well through the Middle Passage, and it would be of value to DeWolf, as he sailed this route frequently. Included was detailed information about the voyage, and since Levi had landed in Havana, he would endeavor to sell the "Articles" for the best price available. Levi stated that he didn't believe he would do that well, perhaps getting no more than the price that was originally paid for his cargo, breaking even.[158] The only sign that the actual cargo on board consisted of slaves would be that the captain mentioned them in his letters while on a journey through the Middle Passage.

The *Semiramis* sailed once again, leaving Bristol in May 1806. James's slaving vessel successfully arrived a few weeks later on the coast of Africa with three captains, Levi, Charles Collins and Charles Slocum. Collins was two years into his assignment as Bristol's collector at the time they sailed. Once there, they purchased 181 slaves and again proceeded on their journey to Cuba. The reality of this voyage is more complex than the letter divulged. The *Semiramis*, although a purported smooth-sailing vessel, had a death-defying journey through the Middle Passage once it left the coast of Africa. During the seventy-four-day passage, 23 slaves perished, which was more than a 12 percent loss of cargo, possibly validating an insurance policy for reimbursement of loss. One excruciatingly long year after departing from Bristol, the *Semiramis* finally landed in Havana in May 1807. There it successfully delivered and sold 158 slaves, confirming Levi's continued involvement in the illegal trade.[159]

Levi DeWolf was brilliantly trained and heavily relied on by older brother James and became an extraordinary contributor toward the family business of trafficking humans. Perhaps the most telling of his valued contribution would be the correspondence Levi sent to James outlining his horrific journey on the *Semiramis*. It is quite likely that he was deeply imbedded in his faith, as was previously mentioned, perhaps as a result of the shame of knowing that what he was involved in left the blood of slaves on his hands. Nevertheless, Levi continued to support his brother in selling captive people into bondage for many years.

Chapter 5

DEWOLF'S NEMESIS

The law stated that it was illegal for <u>any</u> citizen of the United States to have <u>any</u>
involvement in the slave trade to or from <u>any</u> foreign place or country.
—Act of Congress, 1794[160]

The 1790s had been a tumultuous decade for DeWolf as he dodged an arrest warrant in Rhode Island by hiding out in the West Indies. Then DeWolf faced a trial in a foreign country for the same offense. He left his family behind for four years, during which time laws restraining the slave trade were strengthened in the United States. Much of DeWolf's misfortune, however, seemed to coincide with the appointment of William Ellery as collector in 1790 at the customhouse in Newport, Rhode Island. Ellery, and the revisions made to slave trade laws, would come to challenge DeWolf for years in his quest to continue the illegal trafficking of humans.

Ellery, born in 1727, had a rich familial and political history and a father who was the first in his family to attend college. The senior Ellery graduated from Harvard in 1722 at the age of fifteen and became a merchant who participated in the slave trade. The Ellery family moved when William was a young child from Massachusetts to Newport, Rhode Island, becoming one of the first families to settle there.[161]

The younger Ellery followed in the family tradition by attending Harvard College and graduating in 1747 at the age of twenty. Begrudgingly, he then became a merchant but, as a professed Christian, refused to participate in the activity of purchasing and selling slaves as his father did.[162] This is also the time when Ellery began to have a growing distaste for the slave trade in general. Ellery searched for the right career for many years and at one time was employed as the clerk for the Rhode Island General Assembly. In 1770, at the age of forty-three, Ellery began to practice law and seemingly found his passion in life. It was then that he made a name for himself as a politician and was active in the Rhode Island Sons of Liberty. Subsequently, in 1776, Ellery became an active member of the Second Continental Congress and, as a representative for Rhode Island, had the prestigious honor of being one of the signers of the Declaration of Independence.[163]

Ellery served in the Continental Congress as the sole Rhode Island delegate until 1780. At the conclusion of his term, Ellery entered Rhode Island politics in Newport as a grass-roots politician. Serving in the local assembly until May 1783, Ellery then ran for a seat in Congress and was successfully elected. This is when Ellery became more vocal regarding his disapproval of the slave trade. While the Land Ordinance of 1785 was being debated, fellow senator Rufus King moved that slavery should be prohibited from the lands mentioned in the ordinance, and Ellery quickly seconded the motion.[164] With Ellery garnering support from King, the local politician began to gain confidence in his crusade to end all aspects of the slave trade, particularly in his home state.

At the end of his term, Ellery returned to Rhode Island in the quest of local service, holding the office of judge of the Supreme Court of Rhode Island, which created the perfect platform for a vocal advocate in support of the abolition of slavery. During his time on the bench, Ellery began to voice his desire to make another transition and was appointed collector of customs in Rhode Island. Ellery chose to focus his efforts on the collectorship, as there were two openings in the state, one in Providence and the other in his hometown of Newport.[165] Although the competition was fierce, President George Washington appointed Ellery the new collector of Newport, where he quickly entrenched himself as a law-abiding advocate for the abolition movement. Ellery's unwavering devotion to the new nation was undoubtedly inspirational to Washington in his pursuit to find a customs collector for the notably rebellious state.[166] Ultimately, this is exactly what led to Ellery's appointment as the first customs collector of the port of Newport under the provisions of the federal Constitution. He served until his death in 1820.

Unfortunately, Ellery would end up with a family member who did not share his ardent passion for abolitionism. His nephew Christopher Ellery followed in his uncle's footsteps and became a senator for Rhode Island in 1801. But that is where the similarities stop. Senator Christopher Ellery was known to be in support of the slave trade and ultimately became a DeWolf ally.[167]

As a collector, Ellery was considered a significant officer of the state and exercised extensive, and noticeable, authority.[168] All vessels that entered or exited Rhode Island, bound for Bristol or any other port in Rhode Island, needed to register at the customhouse in Newport under Ellery's supervision. Ellery was well informed of the legendary slaving activities of DeWolf and others in the local community and throughout the state. The conscientious collector, who had a commitment to abolition, did everything within his legal power to stop traders from their chosen profession and from cheating the new government out of badly needed revenue.[169] In fact, Ellery became acutely aware that DeWolf's vessels regularly broke multiple laws.

Among Ellery's responsibilities as collector was his communication with government port surveyor and Bristol resident Samuel Bosworth. The responsibilities of a port surveyor involved the investigation of accidents, violations of maritime laws, inspections, verifications of insurance and measurements of ships to determine their tonnage, as required by federal law. He also monitored the comings and goings of ships and crew. The surveyor assumed the responsibility of the collector when the collector could not be present, particularly to determine if a ship was compliant with local, national and/or international shipping laws.[170] Bosworth acted as Ellery's eyes in Bristol, reporting any suspicious activities regarding all vessels registered there, both before and after they reported to the customhouse in Newport.

On June 16, 1794, Ellery sent a letter to Bosworth with specific instructions outlining the Act of 1794. Ellery told Bosworth to be vigilant that this act was not violated—ever.[171] At the age of seventy-two, Ellery depended heavily on the younger Bosworth to assess any illegal activity regarding the slave trade in the port of Bristol.

Once DeWolf finally arrived home in Bristol from the West Indies in 1795, he did not waste any time reestablishing himself as a visibly prominent capitalist in his community. DeWolf had successfully run his business, turning a large profit, from the comfort of an isolated island for four years. Two days after his arrival home, DeWolf received a letter from his uncle Simeon Potter with new advice on how to circumvent the most recent slaving laws. Potter advised DeWolf to go straight to Georgia to sell his slaves to avoid breaking the Act of 1794. Potter stated that this would ensure he received the highest price for his slaves and recommended that DeWolf hire an agent.[172] There were explicit updated directions in this letter regarding the procedure for selling slaves in the southern states. Clearly, his uncle's input regarding the laws that had been put into place during DeWolf's absence would be valuable in expediting his ability to continue slaving from his home port, all the while avoiding further trouble.

With the ratification of the Act of 1794, Rhode Island slavers placed themselves in double jeopardy by continuing to outfit their vessels for slaving and participating in the slave trade to foreign nations.[173] However, the trade defiantly remained active in the state of Georgia, which created a coveted loophole for DeWolf to continue slaving, despite the diligent efforts by Collector Ellery and the laws passed by Congress.

That same year, DeWolf was aware that the laws in Spain still allowed the foreign slave trade to exist and began to pursue a new strategy. Staying one step ahead of the law, DeWolf would frequently register his vessels with Spanish papers, employ Spanish crews and fly the Spanish flag in order to pursue his business under a legal slaving status. At this time, Cuba was a Spanish territory and provided a financially lucrative location for DeWolf's operation. Despite the Act of 1794, DeWolf continued selling slaves in Havana and in various ports in the southern United States. The law generally did not have much impact on the multitude of domestic slave traders, and as a result, few convictions were recorded.[174] Spain resisted abolition in Cuba because of the tremendous need for slaves on its sugar and coffee plantations. This drew heavy traffic into the ports of Havana and Matanzas for slave traders; it also inspired DeWolf to invest in three separate plantations of his own.[175]

Despite the new impediments that DeWolf faced, he became more powerful than ever. On December 4, 1795, his ship the *Juno* sold seventy-five slaves valued at $19,390 at an undisclosed location in the West Indies. Then, on January 9, 1796, this same ship landed in Havana and sold the remaining slaves from the same voyage, valued at $25,105. The next entry on the ship log for that year showed that DeWolf subcontracted with thirty-five different individuals to fulfill their requests for slaves. This exhibits an incessant need to obtain free labor at any cost, even illegally. DeWolf typically charged an average $40 consignment fee for each slave ordered, to be delivered to the original requester, along with a 5 percent commission paid for the value of the slave at the time of arrival.[176] For example, if a slave were purchased for $500, DeWolf's fee was $40 plus his 5 percent commission on the $500, which equaled $20. The person who ordered the slave from DeWolf would pay him $560.

Like other slave captains, DeWolf's ship logs typically listed slaves on board by gender and age instead of physical condition.[177] However, on one terribly costly voyage in 1796, DeWolf became candidly descriptive, as demonstrated in the entry for sixteen of the slaves he transported and the condition they were in once he arrived in port: "3 slaves were dead on arrival, 1 was near death, 2 were very ill, 2 were sick, 1 was very weak, 2 had become very thin, 1 was too old, 2 were very young, 1 very small, 1 had to be carried off the ship."[178]

When several of the aforementioned slaves died, DeWolf was later heard stating that the mortality of cargo resulted in the biggest threat to

A sketch of the vessel *Juno*, commissioned by DeWolf. This is an accurate depiction of a vessel from this time period. Circa 1790s, location of original sketch and artist unknown. *Photo taken by author with permission, Bristol Historical and Preservation Society.*

the financial bottom line and that the mortality of those slaves had ruined the voyage for him.[179] That particular voyage slowly disintegrated as they sailed through the Middle Passage. However, the experience that DeWolf encountered on the *Juno* appeared to be an isolated event, as there is no further mention of him personally having such a catastrophic voyage in his lifetime of slaving.

By 1799, the federal government ruled that if a person was caught transporting slaves, it did not constitute enough evidence for a conviction, lessening the possibility of arrest even further.[180] This certainly had to do with the inability of the United States to support the maritime laws that had been ratified by Congress. The political climate could allow change to be thwarted, just as easily as strengthened, which can be seen in the loosening of the 1799 legislation. DeWolf continued to maintain a strong defiance of the laws, not changing his routine, seemingly unaffected despite the loosening of the legislation. After DeWolf's return to Rhode Island in 1795, a reenergized businessman emerged. His enterprises began booming, and local discussion emerged regarding the need for a third customhouse in the state.

DeWolf had to contend with the legal regulations of Newport's customhouse, which Ellery was increasingly determined to enforce. Shortly upon his return to Bristol, DeWolf became aware that his competitor John Brown had decided to run for political office.[181] In 1798, Brown ran a successful campaign for a seat in the U.S. House of Representatives for the state of Rhode Island. Immediately upon his win, Brown began working on legislation that promoted the building of a third customhouse and another revenue district for the tiny state.[182] Bristol was the proposed location—a highly accessible port for both Brown and DeWolf.[183]

Brown's request was approved, but until a new customhouse could be built, all vessels, including those owned by DeWolf, continued to register in Newport and had to contend with Collector Ellery.[184] Although Ellery had been ineffective up to this point in stopping most slaving vessels, DeWolf certainly must have been concerned that the collector would become more powerful given the fact that the law remained on his side.

Collectors are appointed by the president and sworn in by Congress. As a collector, one is responsible for upholding the law, both domestic and internationally. This was difficult to achieve, as the U.S. government did not allocate resources to enforce laws related to the slave trade.[185] This, in part, had to do with the limited size of the U.S. naval fleet, which held six frigates in 1794 and was greatly outnumbered by slaving vessels.[186] Slavers such as

Brown and DeWolf were well aware of the weaknesses in the enforcement of laws related to the trade.

Customhouses charged revenue that was garnered for both local and federal funding. Districts were determined by population and divided up accordingly. Brown's petition for the creation of yet another revenue district for Rhode Island and a new customhouse ensured continued financial stability for the state and helped increase accessibility at the ports for his ships. It also confirmed the profound number of vessels that sailed in and out of Rhode Island.

From Ellery's perspective, the new customhouse in Bristol was viewed as an added asset in the quest to halt the illegal slave trade activity in the central part of the state, particularly with the appointment and added support of a new law-abiding collector. At the same time, DeWolf also saw how he would benefit, not only from the convenient location, but also because he would no longer need to contend with the Ellery-controlled customhouse in Newport. Both men could independently see an advantageous situation unfolding before them.

Eventually, it would be DeWolf who would benefit enormously from Brown's achievement in the building of the new customhouse at Bristol.[187] And although at the outset Ellery had all of the added support he needed, his battle against slave traders was about to become larger and more active than before.

Chapter 6

INDIANS AND KIDNAPPING

Instantly, eight men dressed as Indians, with faces blackened, ran out from the
crowd abducting the surveyor.[188]
—*Bristolian lore*

William Ellery corresponded regularly with David Barnes, the U.S. attorney for Rhode Island. Barnes endeavored to support Ellery in his efforts to uphold the law by disseminating vital information to him regarding various vessels registered in Rhode Island and their illegal activities. On May 11, 1799, Barnes wrote to Ellery to discuss a ship that was sold on the Caribbean island of St. Thomas to a Danish burgher and registered as such in the local customhouse. The vessel was originally owned and then sold by DeWolf. The ship sat in the West Indies port for a few weeks but was eventually delivered to Captain Slocum in Rhode Island. Interestingly, Slocum was a captain employed by DeWolf. Additionally, it was common practice and well known for DeWolf to be financially vested in many vessels. Slocum's new acquisition received financial backing from DeWolf, with the agreement that he would be a silent partner and receive a percentage of each voyage's profit.[189]

In 1799, a state-of-the-art and recently built schooner was tied up at the DeWolf warehouse in Bristol waiting to be fitted out for its next voyage. DeWolf's nephew, Charles DeWolf, officially owned the ship with brothers James and William DeWolf as financial backers.[190] The captain of this schooner, the *Lucy*, was Charles Collins, future collector of Bristol.[191]

The *Lucy* had been in the Bristol port for only one week when, on July 8, Collector Ellery declared that it was a suspected slaver and impounded the vessel. Ellery charged that the *Lucy* represented a breach in the law prohibiting traffic in slaves, as it was being used as a slaving vessel.[192] This allowed the U.S. District Court in Providence, under the Act of 1794, to condemn the vessel to be sold at auction. The profits from the sale would benefit the federal government. Ellery ordered Surveyor Bosworth to attend the government auction and to bid on the *Lucy* on behalf of the U.S. Treasury. It was believed that by selling this ship, significant revenue would be brought to the area, since slave ships were highly coveted vessels known to be smooth and quick sailing.[193] Bosworth was a longtime Bristol resident who knew the power of the DeWolfs. Being quite familiar with the DeWolfs' influence in town, Bosworth pleaded with Ellery to name someone else to attend to what he described as a distressing business.[194]

However, Ellery denied Bosworth's request and told the surveyor to follow through with his assignment. Ellery had already explained to Bosworth the seriousness of the law and the urgent need to uphold it, as well as how much he depended on Bosworth to follow through with his assignment.[195] Attending the auction was unsettling for Bosworth. At the very least, it would have been uncomfortable since he lived in the same community as DeWolf. Additionally, Bosworth was married to Marshall Peck's niece Elizabeth, and her nephew was married to DeWolf's niece Ann Nancy Bradford. Assuredly, DeWolf was aware of this familial connection, but it is unknown if Ellery was aware of this, which would certainly have created a heightened fear for Bosworth.[196]

As the date of the auction approached, Bosworth tried to keep his assignment a secret. However, in the small town of Bristol, conversation was alive with rumors of threats regarding the impending sale of the DeWolf schooner as crew members remained temporarily unemployed. Collins and DeWolf attempted to persuade Bosworth to defy Ellery's orders and to not attend the auction. Bosworth, after much pressure by local residents, again begged Ellery to release him from this assignment. Ellery declined, demanding that Bosworth attend the sale of the *Lucy* and place a bid for the ship on behalf of the government.[197]

Allegedly, the night before the auction, Bosworth heard an unexpected knock at his door. James and Charles DeWolf and John Brown stood before him, Brown having made a special trip from Providence. They attempted to dissuade Bosworth from attending the auction the next day, insisting that his involvement was not a requirement of his job and would place him in a compromised state in the community. The underlying threat probably frightened Bosworth, who instantly declined their request, shutting the door. Brown returned to Providence, but the surveyor received yet another visit the following morning from James DeWolf, who most decidedly had begun to panic. Making one last attempt to convince Bosworth to stay away from the auction, DeWolf insisted that the sailors at the wharf were so agitated that he could not guarantee the surveyor's safety. Bosworth again declined, stating that he intended to see his assignment through.[198]

The morning of the auction, DeWolf became more determined than ever to purchase and reacquire the *Lucy*. This appeared to have been his plan all along, as DeWolf and his family decided to take matters into their own hands. On the day of the auction and impending sale of the now locally famous schooner, a crowd gathered at the wharf to witness the show. Although many people attended, the only financially viable participants who could purchase the schooner were the DeWolfs and the U.S. government.[199]

A story of that fateful day has been retold to multiple generations of DeWolfs and the community of Bristol. It states that as Bosworth approached the wharf, Collins, who remained hidden in a nearby doorway, waved his hat as a signal. This would not be too conspicuous, for Collins's modest home sat within sight of the harbor. It has been stated that once the signal was given, eight men dressed as Indians, with faces blackened, ran out from the crowd and abducted the surveyor. As Bosworth was physically dragged to a small sailboat tied to the wharf, he called out for help, but no one came.[200] The "Indians" blindfolded Bosworth and paddled him south and east of Bristol Harbor around a point. They then headed north along the shoreline, away from the auction. Bosworth was deposited in a wooded area at the foot of the famed Mount Hope, home of DeWolf patriarch Mark Anthony, a little more than two miles from the auction. It was just far enough to keep Bosworth from walking back in a timely manner.[201] While this tale has been told for generations, it was not repeated to glorify the act but to emphasize the overwhelming power and influence of the DeWolfs.

While Bosworth's abduction did occur, as confirmed by the federal government, the story of an Indian raid is most likely exaggerated local lore. Less than one month after the incident, Bosworth received a letter dated August 5, 1799, from Oliver Wolcott, secretary of the Treasury Department. The letter acknowledged Bosworth's removal from the auction against his will, his false imprisonment and subsequent absence from the auction of the *Lucy*. Wolcott then requested that Bosworth forward any circumstantial details that might help find the instigators of this attack.[202] It is not likely

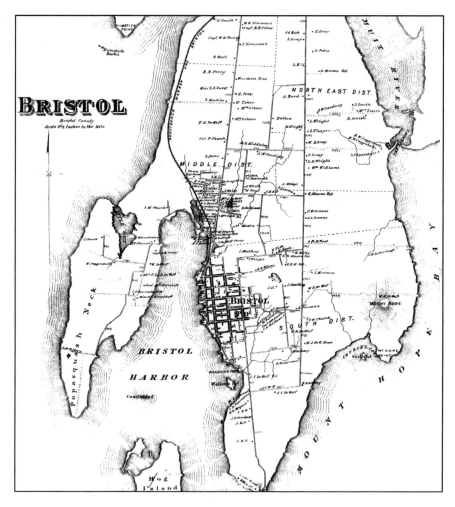

Aerial map of Bristol Harbor, the town and the surrounding area, including Mount Hope, which was owned by family patriarch Mark Anthony DeWolf. *D.G. Atlas of Rhode Island, 1870.*

that Bosworth complied; perhaps he was fearful of further harassment by the ever-powerful DeWolf family, but most likely it was because he was also doing business with DeWolf.

Consequently, back at the port in Bristol, the auction was delayed for as long as the agent dared while awaiting Bosworth's return. Eventually, the agent started the auction as the crowd turned restless. Under the direction of James, the family bid on their own ship, and with Bosworth out of the way,

Samuel Bosworth was doing business with, and owed money to, DeWolf at the time of the auction of the *Lucy. Photo taken by author, with permission from the Bristol Historical and Preservation Society.*

they faced no competition. Whenever a government-seized vessel was put up for auction, although exasperating, owners typically repurchased their vessels for a trivial fraction of their original value. According to Ellery, there were few citizens who dared bid against an influential merchant such as DeWolf. It seemed that by common consent, the local gentlemen refused to bid against one another.[203] This, of course, made government auctions more of a nuisance than a monetary success.

Both DeWolf and Collins recognized that once the bidding began, they needed to have at least two people to place an offer on the ship for the auction to proceed. To give the impression that there was a bidding war, DeWolf secretly enlisted one of his Spanish captains, who remained unknown in Bristol, to place an offer on his behalf. This tactical move ensured the return of the schooner to the DeWolf family.[204] It would have been suspicious if DeWolf and Collins, the former captain of the *Lucy*, had appeared to fight against each other at this auction. The Spanish captain was allowed the final offer to keep DeWolf's name off the registry; however, DeWolf remained the silent owner of the *Lucy*.[205] The vessel immediately resumed its voyages in the slave trade, but where it had previously sailed under the flag of the United States, it now sailed under the Spanish flag, avoiding any further legal complications as an American vessel.

The Treasury Department gained only a paltry $738 from the auction of the *Lucy* in July 1799.[206] With his embarrassing defeat, Ellery seemed momentarily to refrain from challenging the powerful Bristol family, as evidenced by a temporary lull in his correspondence regarding their circumvention of slave trading laws. Ellery instead redirected his efforts in his letter writing campaign to that of evasion of maritime law in general.

Not too long after the unsuccessful auction of DeWolf's vessel, Ellery wrote to Barnes and explained yet another avenue of how the owners of slave vessels manipulated the law, even if their ship's were impounded and put up for public auction. Captains would encourage their crew to go to the auction and explain to the marshal in charge that they had not received any of their wages and that the result of the auction should be to, first, garner enough money to pay them for their service. If the vessel was to be sold, the amount owed for the vessel itself could then be evaded, as the money made from the sale of the vessel was to be used for unpaid wages, conveniently equal to the same amount the vessel was sold for.[207] Ellery's frustration at yet another attempt to keep auction money from going to the U.S. government and the failure of a successful auction was mounting, not to mention the demonstrative disregard DeWolf had for the law.

By November 1799, Barnes had written to Ellery to confirm that it was immaterial who the owners were of the vessels that continued to participate in the slave trade from the United States. It was clear that Ellery's primary efforts were focused on the DeWolf family. Barnes outlined, and confirmed what Ellery already knew, that any American citizen sailing on any vessel, domestic or foreign, that came into port was obliged to give a bond under the Act of 1794. By giving a bond, the captain demonstrated recognition of the slave trade laws and that he and his vessel were not illegal participants.[208] Such a simplistic task was rarely fulfilled if the vessel was determined to maintain an active role in the buying and selling of slaves. The creative nature of DeWolf, and others, who circumvented the law had become more than Ellery could contend with.

Legal obstacles to the slave trade began to accelerate as a result of the Federal Slave Trade Act of 1800; the changes in the country remained on Ellery's side. This law was written to reinforce the largely ignored law of 1794 and reinforce the reality that U.S. citizens were barred from participation in the trade.[209] Coincidentally, this was the same year that DeWolf's coveted customhouse in Bristol finally opened. But before leaving office, then-president John Adams made a midnight appointment of the collector for the newly opened customhouse. Not surprisingly, given Adams's antislavery sentiments, he selected Jonathon Russell, a law-abiding abolitionist, to fill this post. This instantly created a new dilemma for DeWolf.[210] He was well aware of the value of having an ally as collector in Bristol. Accordingly,

DeWolf began a long and arduous three-year struggle to have Russell removed. DeWolf's influence and power became increasingly threatened as antislaving laws stiffened and, to ensure their enforcement, antislavery Federalists were appointed to positions of power.

The new customhouse was built less than one block from Bristol Harbor, a prime location on Narragansett Bay on the northwest side. It even displays some of the same granite that was used on the DeWolf warehouse. The harbor is nearly waterlocked, with an expanse of sheltered, deep water convenient to vessels coming and going. This large body of water begins at the Atlantic Ocean, which flows past the Rhode Island landmass just west of the coastal town of Newport. There are three main bodies of water that bypass Newport and collectively funnel into the main portion of the bay. Two waterways are west of the town of Newport, and one runs just to the east. Originally, slavers would choose the waterway most conducive to the safe delivery of their illegal cargo.

As Rhode Island slave laws evolved and the demand for slaves in the South grew, vessels were illegally outfitted to carry slaves, which required them to continue to sail discreetly in and out of the bay. This pattern continued with every voyage leaving the port of Bristol that knowingly broke the law. The waterway south of Newport, where Ellery was stationed, was typically used. This particular passage was visually protected by a small island that allowed slaving captains to sail inland, easily circumventing the prying eyes of the collector. As a result of its prime location, Narragansett Bay, and the sea, became the dominant element in supporting the Rhode Island economy.[211]

Perhaps observing John Brown's success, and likely motivated by the ever-tightening slave trade restrictions in 1800, DeWolf ran for reelection in the General Assembly of Rhode Island on the Jeffersonian ticket. Brown, who belonged to the opposing Federalist Party, wrote a letter to a friend just prior to the election reminding him that DeWolf was an untried murderer. Brown stated:

> *I wish it may properly be introduced to Mr. James DeWolf that it already begins to be talked of in our streets that if he don't [sic] conduct himself within the bounds of reason, the statement of his murdering his negroes in the smallpox to preserve the other part of his cargo in his passage from Africa will be echoed through the papers of the various states.*[212]

Despite their commonalities regarding involvement in the slave trade, their political tensions were impenetrable. Brown and DeWolf, members of

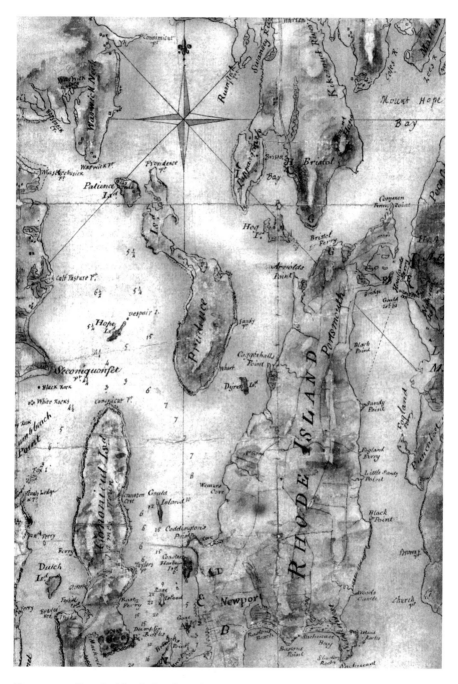

Narragansett Bay, the islands therein and Bristol Harbor, to the right of the Compass Rose. Located at bottom center is Newport. Pen-and-ink watercolor by Charles Blaskowitz, 1777. *Courtesy of the Library of Congress, digital call number Gm71000684.*

the newly emerging opposing parties, must have felt a tremendous personal divide. Brown's attack had little impact on DeWolf, who triumphed in his campaign. At this point, DeWolf took advantage of his renewed political position by diligently petitioning Jefferson, who had just won the presidency, to appoint a new collector at the port of Bristol.[213]

Many have questioned whether DeWolf, and others, broke the law when they outfitted their vessels specifically for the transport and selling of slaves. It is not uncommon to hear the expression "that's just what they did back then." Yet the law remained in place, despite the blatant disregard many exhibited, and violations of the law can be seen in the volumes of correspondence from those who vainly attempted enforcement. This ignorant perspective allowed for a level of denial in regards to the laws put into place by both local and federal governments. It was a reckless response to the gruesome reality of the poor souls who were subjected to imprisonment as a result of the greed that so blatantly drove the trade.

Chapter 7

POLITICS

[Speaking of President Jefferson:] *Consider the political advantages the party would gain should he choose to remove Federalist appointees in their state… down with the Tories!*[214]
—*Charles Collins, 1803*

During his run for office, James DeWolf had simultaneously campaigned as a vocal and influential supporter of Thomas Jefferson's presidential candidacy. This was something of a risk for DeWolf; Jefferson's Republican ideology angered many locally and domestically, as it promoted an even more egalitarian political system in the United States. Jefferson's forward thinking allowed the opportunity for the common man to be involved in legislative reapportionment. This was a progressive way of thinking compared to the Federalists. As a rule, the Federalist Party advocated a strong central government, maintaining a pessimistic view regarding the common man's contributions and abilities to participate intelligently in the political process. It believed that the government should resist the passions of the general public and rely solely on a small group of governing elite.[215] Jefferson's ultimate goal was to promote the common good by establishing a government run by the best minds. Educational advantages and high social status would no longer be the sole determining factors.[216] Rhode Island, at the time, was a strong Federalist state that heavily resisted change. Most New Englanders regarded Jefferson as a dangerous radical, if not the devil incarnate.[217] This accounted, in part, for Brown's aggressive public attack against DeWolf's campaign.

Using his influence in many communities throughout the state to help Jefferson gain much-needed support, DeWolf actively lobbied for Jefferson and his inexperienced Republican Party.[218] The public visibility that DeWolf achieved while supporting Jefferson throughout Rhode Island also provided the significant exposure he needed for his personal campaign. The benefits derived from DeWolf's successful political election and the support he gave to Jefferson were part of a well-calculated plan to court the president. This culminated in 1801, when DeWolf named one his vessels the *Thomas Jefferson*. It also resulted in a brilliantly conceived turn of opportunism for DeWolf.[219]

Jefferson's win brought a new political philosophy to the nation. George Washington's original course of action advocated that there should be no division within the country based on political parties and that all political goals of this nation should remain as one.[220] Despite this warning, Jefferson and Adams created national division, and their parties grew up around them. Because Adams felt that only members of his political party should be appointed into positions of power, several midnight appointments were made during his final hours as president. This ensured that only Federalists would be left in highly coveted offices once Jefferson was sworn into the presidency.[221] All of the appointees chosen held the same political views as Adams. This instantly created concern for President-elect Jefferson and his new political ideals. Once Jefferson took office, Republicans urgently encouraged him to begin work immediately on reversing Adams's last-minute appointments.[222]

In the first few months of his presidency, appointments and removals occupied most of his time. As he methodically went through lists of nominees for his consideration, Jefferson noted in a letter written on April 8, 1801, to Archibald Stuart of Virginia that there was nothing he was more anxious to do than place good people into positions presently held by Federalists. Jefferson also stated that he was conscious that the merit, as well as the reputation, of a good administration depended as much on his choices as on its measures.[223]

As Jefferson took the presidential oath of office in 1801, DeWolf was sworn in as a new member of the Rhode Island General Assembly. It was shortly thereafter that the slaver began to deliberately plan revenge against William Ellery and his attacks on the DeWolf family empire. Once the customhouse in Bristol was opened, it was placed under the supervision of the state collector. To undermine Ellery's influence, DeWolf first petitioned Jefferson to have the port of Bristol become a revenue district independent of the state collector. The second phase of DeWolf's plan was to have Jonathon Russell replaced by his brother-in-law, Charles Collins. DeWolf was accustomed to having instantaneous results regarding his efforts toward personal gain. Certainly, he could not have anticipated the lengthy delay in fulfilling his second request—it took nearly three years before Collins was sworn in to his new position.[224]

DeWolf had ulterior motives for choosing Collins as the candidate for collector of Bristol. Collins was not only related to DeWolf by marriage, but he was also a captain and part owner of two slaving vessels, the *Amastad* [sic] and the *Minerva*. Furthermore, between the years 1789 and 1799, Collins captained a minimum of seven slaving voyages. At least four were on ships owned by DeWolf.[225]

As a captain, Collins had a particularly bad year in 1797, in which he personally lost two vessels due to bad weather while they were sailing through the Middle Passage. During this time, Collins and Levi DeWolf were on a third vessel owned by DeWolf that landed in St. Thomas. Once they arrived, Collins wrote about the fate of his two ships to DeWolf, who was an investor, and what he and Levi had arranged in order to successfully move forward. There is no mention in his letter of the fate of his crew or the cargo of slaves who would have been on board. While in St. Thomas, Collins purchased seven Negroes, the required number to qualify for entry into Havana, and then both Collins and Levi proceeded on to Cuba together. Because of Collins's personal loss, he declared with some urgency in his correspondence to DeWolf the need to arrive in Havana as quickly as possible. Collins was determined to make up some of his loss by taking advantage of the current sugar prices.[226]

Six years after the unfortunate loss of both of Collins's vessels, in October 1803, DeWolf and his brother John sent Collins, along with a contingent of Republicans from Rhode Island, to Washington, D.C. The ambitious nature of this trip, made with exuberant optimism, was to meet with President Jefferson. The motivation for this meeting was to readdress the topic of a new appointment for the customhouse in Bristol.[227]

After his arrival in the capital on October 22, 1803, Collins penned a lengthy letter to John DeWolf, giving a detailed report of his visit. In it, he stated that he initially met with Senator Christopher Ellery of Rhode Island in the senator's chambers once Congress adjourned for the day. Christopher Ellery, nephew of Rhode Island's collector William Ellery, was also a slaver, which most certainly was disheartening to his uncle. Collins wrote that he asked Senator Ellery for advice on how to proceed with the president regarding the replacement of the collector at Bristol. Collins stated that the senator concurred and was entirely supportive; he claimed it was an absolute necessity to remove not only the collector but also all of the Tory officers (Federalists) throughout the United States.[228]

Tory was a term used by individuals to describe a person who exhibited betrayal of the worst kind, going against all national interests. The word was used as an odious epithet in conversation and is demonstrated as such in Thomas Paine's inspirational pre-Revolutionary pamphlet, *Common Sense*. Throughout the American Revolution, supporters of the British Crown were commonly referred to as Tories, and nearly thirty years later, the term was still widely used.

After he spoke with the senator, Collins gave it as his opinion that the Republican members from Rhode Island should meet with the president to convey their evaluation in regards to Bristol's customhouse appointment.[229] Furthermore, the letter indicated that the senator then arranged a meeting between Jefferson, Collins and the Rhode Island Republican contingent. While meeting with Jefferson, according to Collins, they

> *informed him that they expected that the Republican part of the Legislation take up the matter* [regarding the removal of Federalists from their positions] *at their next session and perhaps petition generally, as there existed a very great uneasiness among the People of the State—so we left him to Chew on it.*[230]

With the "People from the Northward…urging a Removal of Officers," the president was now forced into a political game of tug-of-war with a persuasive group of supporters who represented a valuable foothold for him in the North. Collins then informed DeWolf that he had done all he could do for the time being in Washington. "Now is the time to send forward a Petition, such as we talked of before I left home," Collins wrote. "Let it be signed by all of the Republican Members of the Legislature and others as you may think fit." Collins stated toward the end of the letter, "Down with the Tories," with a noticeably bold strike of the pen.[231]

During his meeting with the northern Republican contingency, Jefferson was initially ambivalent about replacing collector Russell. However, after much pressure, he began to realize the value of wealthy friends in the Republican Party from the still hostile state of Rhode Island. Before they returned home, Collins and the others left one final thought for Jefferson, urging him to consider the political advantages the party would gain should he choose to remove Federalist appointees in their state. This would further underscore the power of party divisions and would ultimately benefit Rhode

Island slavers.[232] The result of this time-consuming adventure proved to be so valuable for DeWolf that it begs the question of whether Jefferson ever regretted the decision he was about to make.

A few short months later, in the early part of 1804 and as a result of continual pressure from the few but highly influential Republicans of Rhode Island, Jefferson appointed and received congressional approval for Collins to replace Russell as Bristol's new collector.[233] This was exactly what DeWolf needed to ensure his unrelenting continuance in the slave trade. There is no doubt that this devastated Collector Ellery. DeWolf had succeeded in protecting his business interests by securing his brother-in-law's appointment as collector from President Jefferson. The DeWolfs made an incredibly bold move sending Collins as part of the Rhode Island contingency, not only to speak with Senator Ellery, but also to speak directly to the president. The ideological stance of Jefferson on the topic of slavery had been so profoundly ambivalent, it was difficult for DeWolf to ignore the opportunity to combine patriotism and profit.[234]

At the time of Collins's appointment, he was sworn to uphold the Constitution and federal laws. Under federal guidelines, collectors were prohibited from engaging in commerce of any nature related to the port, as it was a conflict of interest. Additionally, the collector's responsibilities were to see that all violators of the law, including those who remained actively involved in the slave trade, were brought to justice.[235] In front of Congress in 1804, Collins was sworn in and promised to uphold the Constitution, which at this time forbade the practice of slaving by any U.S. citizen, particularly federal employees. The very day Collins officially became collector, his slaving vessel the *Minerva* landed in Havana with 150 slaves, breaking the law of 1800 that barred U.S. citizens from exporting slaves to *any* country.[236] Moreover, Collins, like DeWolf, purchased after his appointment a profitable sugar plantation just outside Matanzas, Cuba, which he operated with the support of slaves. Collector Collins boldly sailed to Cuba every year on one of his own vessels to check on his crops, slaves and the business of his estate.[237]

His appointment was clearly disastrous for antislavery supporters and the enforcement of antislaving laws in Rhode Island. It was also a clear example of DeWolf's calculated ability to continue in the trade by further manipulating the system in his favor. Collins received a letter in March, 1804 from the Treasury Department issuing final instructions regarding his position as collector and issuing a bond in Collins's name for the sum of $2,000. The bond was government insurance protecting the customhouse, and Collins, in the event someone in the public sector accused him of participating in any

Collins's first home (1780) was modest compared to the mansion he built twenty-five years later using illicit income. *Photo taken by author.*

Collins's home built in 1805 with proceeds from the slave trade, as DeWolf's business partner and Bristol's customhouse collector. *Photo taken by author.*

illegal activity—which, surprisingly, no one did.[238] Collins remained involved in the slave trade while acting as collector, maintaining ownership of his two very active slaving vessels, which he himself had captained. After Collins assumed office, Senator Ellery sent a letter of confirmation to DeWolf in which he wrote, "There is now dear Sir, nothing more to be done for Bristol—everything which she asked is granted."[239]

Rhode Island slavers found that they could now take advantage of the new collector by sailing upstream, past Newport, into Narragansett Bay, arriving at the port of Bristol without the threat of being questioned about their professional motives.[240] If a threat arose that made it necessary for a DeWolf vessel to sail under Spanish colors, Collector Collins arranged a fabricated sale of the ship to his personal Cuban agent.[241] DeWolf not only had an extra set of eyes watching out for his fleet in Bristol, but he also had the opportunity to continue sailing under the Spanish flag if he felt it was necessary, always staying a step ahead of authorities.

Evidence shows that ships sailing in and out of the port of Bristol headed for the coast of Africa more than doubled after Collins's appointment. This was true for DeWolf, too, as he logged twenty-one voyages between 1799 and 1803 under the first collector and at least forty-two from 1804 until the end of the year in 1807, more than doubling his profits. DeWolf continued to circumvent slave trade laws with ease. From this moment, there were no more documented attempts at prosecutions in Rhode Island for breaking the law on trading slaves until the end of 1807.[242]

Despite the ratification of the Act of 1800, Bristol remained one of the top three slave trade ports in America, yet it does not find itself in a prominent place in the history of the United States. Along with Newport, Bristol exported slaves to the active port of Charleston, South Carolina, well past the end of 1807. Many pages of DeWolf's correspondence would confirm a much later date before it stopped.[243]

William Ellery vainly attempted to work with his new collector in Bristol. Ellery again sent correspondence, this time to Collins, regarding a vessel preparing to evade the embargo that originated from his port. Ellery's correspondence stated that it was reported that many crew members were told to say goodbye to their families and did not know when they would return. The crew members also neglected to discuss where they would be traveling to and for what purpose. The only additional information given was the name of the vessel: *Sally*. Although there were multiple vessels named *Sally*, there was only one known from the port of Bristol; it was owned by DeWolf's nephew George and financially backed by DeWolf. Ellery then concluded in his letter that he would advise Collins to be certain not to allow any vessel to depart from Bristol without verifying the ballast and then collecting a bond to ensure that the voyage was of legal nature. A legal bond issued by Collins as collector was not uncommon. However, the vessels that routinely received these bonds were small and used for the sole purpose of transporting goods domestically within his jurisdiction in rivers, bays and sounds. Collins neglected to collect bonds for many of the larger vessels that actually exited Bristol Harbor into Narragansett Bay to sail for the open seas toward unknown destinations for unexplained reasons.[244]

Although Collins secured the position of collector for the port of Bristol and was sworn to uphold the law, he not only continued to be personally involved in the trade, but evidently he was also available to be placed on a financial retainer to look the other way. Looking at James DeWolf's personal bankbook from the Bank of Bristol, DeWolf wrote entries stating debits to be made directly to Collins every even month, for six payments per year, beginning in 1807. The last entry noted was June 20, 1811, as this was the last bankbook that could be found. The possibility of these payments continuing is quite strong; the probability that they were used to ensure discretion is feasible.[245]

Chapter 8

SLAVE TRADE ACCELERATES

Kidnapped as young children, Pauledore and Adjua were forced to marry one another when they came of age, in the parlor of Mrs. DeWolf, and remained married and in her "employ" until the day they died.
—DeWolf family lore

The slaving business accelerated shortly after 1800 with the anticipation of the federal government constitutionally banning the slave trade altogether in 1808. The proposed law promised new and heightened penalties unlike previous laws. The fines for someone convicted of slaving began in the thousands of dollars and included a prison sentence.[246] Disregarding the federal law, DeWolf continued to dispatch vessels for the sole purpose of buying and selling slaves, many of whom were delivered to the newly reopened ports in South Carolina. DeWolf would go to great lengths to circumvent slaving laws, including the falsification of records. Two examples of his cunning ability to evade the authorities can be seen on the manifests from both the *Minerva* and the *Amastad*.[247] Absurdly, both vessels were financially backed by DeWolf and owned by federally appointed Collector Collins in Bristol.

The *Amastad* left Bristol on November 22, 1802, with Cadiz listed as its destination in order to circumvent the Act of 1800.[248] However, this vessel sailed to the coast of Africa.[249] The ship was captained by a Spaniard named Juan Jose Mantonell. This was another tactical move, as Spain had yet to enact a law stopping the slave trade. This encouraged DeWolf and others to eventually purchase working plantations in Spanish-controlled Cuba. Several items listed on the ship's log were intended for sale or trade, valued at $19,815. Multiple hogsheads of rum, the main commodity to trade for slaves, were included on the manifest and were listed with a value of $14,316.[250]

The *Minerva* left the port of Bristol five days after the *Amastad*, on November 27, 1802. This vessel also avoided listing Africa as its destination by indicating that it would sail to Barbados, once again bypassing the law of 1800. DeWolf hired William Collins, son of the collector, to captain this voyage. This particular manifest avoided listing items that would be sold or traded but instead listed food items, most of which would have been consumed by the crew on its passage to Africa.[251]

Both of these DeWolf ships sailed to the coast of Africa instead of the destinations noted on the ships' manifests, violating the Slave Trade Act of 1794 and the revised acts to strengthen it thereafter. As mentioned earlier, these laws explicitly stated that U.S. citizens were prohibited to transport slaves to the United States or any foreign country, including Cuba, as well as prohibited to outfit a ship for the purpose of slaving.[252]

Congressional leaders persevered in their efforts to modify the slave trade laws, but it was a vain attempt to stop the trafficking of humans by such individuals like DeWolf. However, despite their increase in penalties if caught transporting slaves or outfitting vessels for the slave trade, there was no substantive means for enforcing the laws. DeWolf, and others like him, were keenly aware of this fact. In 1803, he captained the *Lavinia* to the coast of Africa, where he acquired 153 slaves.[253]

Also in 1803, the antislaving state law of 1792 was repealed in South Carolina, giving a green light to fulfill the insatiable demand for slaves throughout the area and reopening its ports.[254] In reality, Charleston had been a port of delivery for slaves despite the state and federal laws that prohibited the trade. But once the law officially allowed slave sales to resume, the port of Charleston quickly filled with competing opportunistic vessels. Rhode Island slavers, who already handled between 80 to 90 percent of the slaves sold throughout the nation, immediately took advantage of this opportunity.[255] Beginning in late 1806 and continuing into 1807, the DeWolfs sent at least eighteen vessels to Charleston carrying a total of nearly 2,300 slaves, if not more, in less than seven months.[256] Curiously, one of the vessels was named the *Monticello*, after Thomas Jefferson's famed estate.[257]

Responding to South Carolina's repeal in 1803, the market soared as traders recognized imports would soon be cut off in five short years. The southern state was concerned about a bill that was being written by Congress; if ratified, the slave trade would be severely threatened with increased penalties to those who were involved. This motivated the temporary repeal in the region. It also inspired DeWolf to form a business partnership with a man in Charleston by the name of Charles Christian.

Taking this opportunity while continuing to work in the General Assembly of Rhode Island, DeWolf arranged for the exclusive sale of slaves from the family's ships to Christian. This shrewd business move took DeWolf's empire to an entirely new level. DeWolf, in partnership with this well-established Charleston merchant, opened a commission house for all of his cargoes, naming the firm Christian and D'Wolf.[258]

DeWolf's nephew Henry oversaw the Charleston business that dealt directly with the slave sales. DeWolf also set up an office in New York to deal with the financial end of the Charleston business. The New York office was run by DeWolf's oldest son, James Jr., or "Gentleman Jim," who waited to honor all financial drafts sent to him by his cousin Henry.[259] This scenario further demonstrated DeWolf's savvy business mind and his ability to expand his already well-developed, vertically integrated empire by utilizing trusted family members. It was clear that James DeWolf had no intention of abandoning the slave trade in the immediate future, despite his active role in state politics.

As anticipated, Jefferson addressed Congress in December 1806, with the challenge to criminalize the slave trade more stringently and stating that it should be put into effect in two short years, on January 1. Congress began to position itself to ratify the newly revised Federal Slave Trade Act of 1808. This law repeated the statute that importing slaves into the United States or its territories was banned. However, the penalties recorded were far more severe, increasing fines ranging from $5,000 to $25,000, forfeiture of the ship and, for the first time, imprisonment from five to ten years for all of the crew. With the Act of 1808 pending in Congress, DeWolf appeared to personally go on one last documented slave voyage to Africa in 1806. The motivation for this voyage was to leave the impression that this powerful politician and businessman intended to abide by the law and quit the trade.

Many historians have stated that DeWolf had not made a voyage for several years because of his age and presumably his election to the General Assembly in Rhode Island, but these assertions came from a family narrative published in 1959. Not only did DeWolf continue to be a hands-on investor, but he also arranged several voyages using his brothers, extended family and captains for hire.

FOR THE PUBLIC.

IT is, at laſt, clearly proved, that it was that long-ſpliced J——— D——— W———, that was the principal in furniſhing the piece from this place, for the Newport Republican, of the 12th ult. the ſame that his Father brags ſo much of, as being a great Politician; but if he had been thrown overboard, at the time the CHILD was thrown out of the Cabin-Window—the Public might have been relieved from the trouble of a great Nuiſance.*

The Scriptures are full of all things that are right,
And often warn mortals not to 'begin the firſt ſtrife;
And to be excepted, I am ſure there is none;
But woe unto the man that throws the firſt ſtone.

Then hail thou Chief, among the B———s!
Don't boaſt ſo much of your genius;
Since Cheſterfield, Voltaire, you prefer
To the advice of Chriſtians.

Great in Virtue, I wiſh you might,
That I may ſing your praiſe;
I would even blackguard for your right,
That you might Virtue prize.

'Twixt Boys, leſs than yourſelf,
This mighty difference look on;
They, to their country, are upright,
But you, to all deception.

A youthful Lad, to Fame unknown,
I dare preſume thou art;
Then why ſo boldly do you write,
When rotten is your heart.

C———.
Now boys and girls are hurried away,
By a ſhilling, or ſomething better:
But the time may come, when onion boys,
Will proclaim veſſels, eſteemed by a Collector.

When, at the appointment, will ſay, Mighty Jeff,
I was much deceived, and wronged;
And ſince ***** introduced him here,
I am glad, he had his Noſe rung.

L———.
The man appears half-ground and light,
Tho' ſome folks think him funny:
But if he had kept his hands ſhut tight,
He would have ſav'd his money.

* There was a veſſel coming from the Coaſt of Africa ſome years ago, and their was a Child born on board; and, whether the Captain was the Father of it, and wiſhed to hide his guilt, by throwing it overboard, is ſtill unknown; however, the Child was undoubtedly thrown out of the Cabin Windows. M. G.
Briſtol, July, 1806.

"For the Public" (1806) states that a slave baby was born on a DeWolf voyage, so he tossed it out the cabin window while at sea. *Photo taken by author, with permission from the Bristol Historical and Preservation Society.*

Choosing to sail again in 1806 at the age of forty-one, and before the revised law was put into place, could perhaps be explained from a variety of perspectives. For this voyage, DeWolf chose to sail on the *Andromache*, said to be his favorite vessel from his private fleet. It was an unusually large ship for that time period, weighing 192 tons with a sixty-two-foot keel.[260] A typical schooner during the late eighteenth/early nineteenth century would average approximately 104 tons.[261] The extra length of the keel provided smooth control and stability in navigating the ship. It boasted a twenty-three-foot beam, which was broader than that found on most vessels at the time and contributed to the stability of the ship—a critical component for sailing through the rough waters often experienced during the Middle Passage. Despite the horrors of the slave trade and arrogance of the slaving business, DeWolf's decision to use the *Andromache* for his alleged last voyage would substantiate the seriousness he took in approaching this well-scripted journey.[262]

The *Andromache*'s voyage is downplayed as a result of Bristol lore. Many have stated that the voyage departed in 1807 and returned just days before Christmas the same year. There is also the claim that DeWolf returned with two young slaves for Mrs. DeWolf as Christmas presents. However, evidence showed the real story to be quite different. DeWolf actually left Bristol on the *Andromache* on June 11, 1806. He sailed directly for Africa, arriving two months later, on August 12. While anchored on the Gold Coast, DeWolf purchased 186 slaves and then set sail for the Carolinas. During his voyage through the Middle Passage, on his way to Charleston, 20 slaves tragically died and were disposed of overboard. In 1807, five months after departing from Africa, the *Andromache* arrived in Charleston. While there, DeWolf sold only 107 slaves, leaving 59 on board.[263]

By April 13, 1807, DeWolf once again set sail, this time departing from Charleston for Cuba. Typically, a voyage would go from the coast of Africa directly to the West Indies or a southern state, returning thereafter to its homeport. Another option would be to stop in Havana; buy and sell items, including slaves; and then sail directly to a port in the United States to do business before returning home. For DeWolf to go to Charleston first and then make Cuba his second stop was unusual. He could have been motivated by the high death rate during transit, which created a loss of revenue. DeWolf arrived in Havana on April 13, 1807, and sold the remaining 59 slaves: 20 men, 13 women, 3 boys, 1 girl, 16 male infants and 6 female infants. He departed for Rhode Island two weeks later, on April 26, 1807.[264] This was four months later than previously documented.[265] The last entry made by DeWolf on the ship's log of the *Andromache* was on September 30, 1807. This suggests the approximate date of arrival back to Bristol and shows his trip took more than 400 days, not 306 as previously claimed.[266] Landing nearly three months before Christmas disputes the claim by the family that he was on a "quick trip."[267] DeWolf's alleged final voyage was deliberately planned, lasted for more than one year and consisted of far more transactions in more locations than previously thought.

It should be noted that the ability to carry infants on board a vessel traveling for months at sea would imply that there were likely a few nursing mothers listed on the manifest. As a result, the nursing mothers would be required to perform the duty of wet nurse to the infants traveling alone. This also gives the impression that DeWolf, too, might have been planning ahead for his plantations in Cuba before the Act of 1808 went into effect.

When DeWolf returned home from his "farewell" voyage, he purportedly brought with him two young slaves who were scooped up off the coastline of Africa. It is claimed, according to family lore, that the slave children came from two separate beaches and two separate African tribes. The girl was named Adjua, pronounced *Agiway*, and the boy was named Pauledore, pronounced *Polydore*.[268] Even recently, historians have recounted the story of the two slave children Mrs. DeWolf supposedly received as gifts from her husband as early as 1803. The notion that two slaves were brought to Mrs. DeWolf as Christmas presents is challenged, as all of the slaves on the manifest were sold.

Reviewing the U.S. federal census records of 1810, DeWolf listed three slaves living in his household.[269] By 1820, however, the census forms had elaborated further on who lived in the household by profession, "Free White" or "Free Colored," with a breakdown by gender and age. DeWolf indicated on his 1820 census form that he now had one "Free Colored Male" between the ages of twenty-six and forty-four, one "Free Colored Female" between the ages of zero and thirteen and one "Free Colored Female" between the ages of twenty-six and forty-four.[270] The ages of the man and woman coincide with the dates of DeWolf's travel on the *Andromache* and the family tale of the young children being delivered to Mrs. DeWolf. However, the children were not young. Adjua was born in 1794, which would make her twenty-six at the time of the 1820 census and, at the time of her abduction, a young teen, around twelve or thirteen. It is presumed that Pauledore was approximately the same age during this time. Therefore, the census report would concede that the children were older than previously stated by family historians or they were taken from their homelands at a much earlier date than previously noted. Either way, the two slaves lived with the DeWolfs, serving as their loyal servants until at least 1837, at which time DeWolf died, followed by his wife, who died less than two weeks later, in 1838.

The story further insisted that the two were married in the parlor of Mrs. DeWolf and had several daughters of their own. Oral histories taken in Bristol repeat this story, and although there is no documentation of the marriage occurring in Mrs. DeWolf's parlor, the two children were recognized as a married couple when they were older and had at least one son and two daughters, according to census records taken in 1830.[271] Additionally, DeWolf family historians have also stated that the DeWolfs had great affection for the two slaves. It seems mysterious that DeWolf would have such fondness for his personal slaves when he presented himself as a cold-hearted man toward the lives of the Africans he bought and sold. The availability for Adjua and Pauledore, as well as others, to be buried in his personal family cemetery does not fit the businessman but perhaps gives a glimpse into the life of the family man. Was he an opportunist, forbearing or a combination of these things? The vastly different relationship DeWolf had with his personal slaves and those he sold for profit was extremely unconventional.

Upon their deaths, it is stated that the two slaves were buried in the DeWolf family cemetery. Originally, family historians recounted that the slaves had been buried inside James's personal tomb, but we know that's not true.[272] Adjua's headstone was found in the DeWolfs' private cemetery in Bristol. Pauledore's has yet to be discovered; however, Bristol residents believe he was buried nearby Adjua's resting place and that the stone has gone missing. When you walk through the gates onto the small grounds of the DeWolf cemetery, you can walk straight ahead or take a path that breaks off to the left. Many of the original descendants of James are buried down the path to the left. If you chose to walk straight ahead, down a long narrow path, on the right side, the stones reveal multiple family members from the past to the present. As you continue past these tombstones and make your way toward a narrow path that eventually reaches the tomb of James and Nancy Ann DeWolf, there is a small clearing on the left where two, possibly three, servants are buried in their own area, separated from the rest.

Adjua died at age seventy-four on March 27, 1868. Her tombstone no longer stands but lays in the presumed place of burial, broken into two pieces. Directly beside it is another marker with the name Judith Honeyman. It was long presumed to be a child's grave, as it was unusually small. However, in the winter of 2013, the stone was raised, cleaned and reset only to confirm that this was, in fact, a third DeWolf slave never mentioned before. Ms. Honeyman died on

March 9, 1831, at the age of seventy. "A Faithful Servant" is boldly inscribed at the bottom of her tombstone.[273]

According to U.S. census records, Pauledore lived eight years longer than his wife. On November 24, 1876, Pauledore died, his exact age unknown. The 1870 census recorded that Pauledore was living with Annie P. Slade and Carrington P. Slade and that all three were listed as black. It is logical to presume that Pauledore lived out his remaining years, after his wife's death, in the home of one of his daughters. However, documentation to confirm this assumption has yet to be found.[274]

Before DeWolf died, he made burial provisions for

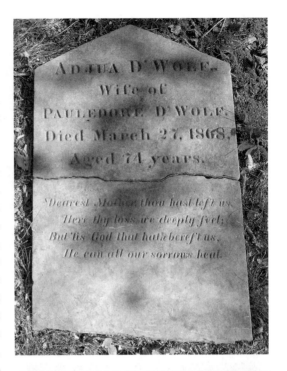

Top: Adjua D'Wolf headstone. "Dearest Mother, thou hast left us, Here thy loss we deeply feel; But 'tis God hath bereft us, He can all our sorrow heal." *Photo taken by author.*

Right: Judith Honeyman. "A Faithful Servant" is inscribed on her headstone. The North transitioned from using the term slave to using servant to comply with newly written laws. *Photo taken by author.*

James and Ann DeWolf's tomb in their private cemetery. The tomb is quite massive but appears reduced as a result of eroding dirt and randomly growing trees and foliage. *Photo taken by author.*

his direct descendants, establishing the cemetery where his tomb stands today. He left explicit instructions that his wife was to be buried with him and that no outsiders or extended family were to be buried in the tomb or within the area designated as the private cemetery.[275] Not surprisingly, with rumors swirling throughout Bristol and the surrounding areas of DeWolf being buried with his riches in gold, there was a robbery of the DeWolf tomb a short five years after the couple's interment. Unfortunately for the thief, John Dickinson, the only negotiable assets that could be found were DeWolf's gold teeth, a handful of gilded buttons from his jacket and the nameplate from the coffin, all of which were sold for $6.52.[276] At the time of this publication, there remains one DeWolf family member who will be allowed to be buried in this small family cemetery, if he chooses.

With DeWolf's well-staged farewell voyage successfully ending in 1807, and before the implementation of the Act of 1808, he convincingly left the impression—at least for his descendants and possibly his contemporaries—that he actually gave up the trade. What still remained in DeWolf's favor was the appointment of his brother-in-law and slaving co-investor to the position of Bristol's collector.

Ironically, at the conclusion of DeWolf's voyage on the *Andromache*, his vessel *Three Sisters* landed on October 12, 1807, in Charleston with a cargo of slaves valued at $29,090. The ledger for this vessel had a clear itemization of who ordered what type of slave by gender, approximate age and quantity needed. There were a total of 106 slaves delivered to 20 people at the port of Charleston. Of the captured men, women, young girls and young boys listed, the largest number was surprisingly young girls, at the count of 46. Two different men on the ledger ordered 29 slaves each. One of those men ordered 18 women in his total of 29. The gender mix purportedly was for forced reproduction purposes, a common practice at the time. It also ensured the continuance of the slave population once the law of 1808 was more strictly enforced.[277]

The *Three Sisters*'s final spreadsheet was tallied with notes regarding cash received and who would pay their balance and when. It was signed by DeWolf's nephew Christian D'Wolf, who himself had ordered one young girl and one young boy.[278] To put this into perspective, $30,000 in the early nineteenth century would have to be multiplied by fifteen to get the twenty-first-century equivalent. Economically, this equals a total of nearly $500,000 for only one of DeWolf's extremely profitable shipments of slaves.[279]

Collins took great risks to support not only DeWolf but also others close to him in the continuance of the slave trade. This contributed to not only DeWolf's continued success regarding the buying and selling of slaves but also the success of all DeWolf family members, including the next generation, far beyond the ratification and implementation of the Act of 1808.

Chapter 9

FRUSTRATION WITH THE LAW

By 1812, President Madison had acquired enough information to once again address Congress regarding the blatant disregard American slavers had for the law…two of the vessels he spoke of were owned by James DeWolf.

The enforcement mechanism that was put into place was compromised in Bristol, and the jurisdiction of the Treasury Department to uphold the law continued to appear helpless.[280] With the passing of the Federal Slave Trade Act of 1808, many Rhode Islanders continued their tenacious fight to ensure that the state's commerce continued through the activities, legal or not, of such families as the DeWolfs. Once again, the government grossly neglected the application of this law, which allowed multiple violations to occur. Contrary to previous assertions, DeWolf and others immediately began planning to circumvent the newly revised regulation.[281] It seemed unlikely that these Bristolian merchants would suddenly agree to find a new form of consistent revenue.

Historiography has stated that DeWolf definitively quit the slave trade at the conclusion of 1807. However, the new slave trade law was written in such a way that there continued to be loopholes that could be used by captains to legitimize their cargo. In fact, this seemed to become hardly a challenge for the most brazen of slavers such as DeWolf. The only adjustment that needed to be made in order to continue in the slaving business after 1808 was to have Africa dropped as the destination on the customhouse ledgers and list only what was transported on board as plain and simple "cargo."[282]

However, the time had arrived to resort to a heightened level of discretion when outfitting vessels with tools for the trade and filing insurance and customhouse paperwork. The last component had already been arranged by DeWolf with the appointment of supportive collector, and fellow slaver, Charles Collins.

The amount of time that DeWolf and Collins would have spent together socially, or discussing business, created an effective bond as close as the DeWolf brothers. In 1797, Collins married Lydia Bradford, sister of DeWolf's wife, Nancy Ann Bradford, at St. Michael's Church. DeWolf and Nancy were married seven years earlier in Bristol at the same church.[283] This relationship promoted lucrative conditions for Collins to be able to predict the movements and decisions made by DeWolf while he was on one of his many slaving vessels. The new collector was an excellent commodity to have at home for DeWolf but, at the same time, a clear threat for the federal government.

As collector for the port of Bristol, Collins maintained an egalitarian policy of obstructionism toward all who opposed the slave trade. This appointment was another cunning business decision and tenacious fighting tactic orchestrated by DeWolf, furthering his ability to participate in the trade. All applications for ships' documents requested by Collector Ellery, particularly for those destined for Africa after the implementation of the act, were ignored by Collins.[284] Ellery repeatedly made unsuccessful requests to Albert Gallatin, secretary of the treasury, for a large naval force to be stationed in Rhode Island to help enforce the Act of 1808. He felt their presence in his state would stop the continuance of illegal trade activity. He was most certainly correct in this assumption; however, neither the secretary nor the federal government ever complied.[285]

Correspondence between the aged Ellery and the U.S. Treasury Department has substantiated that DeWolf and his family continued slaving after 1808. Within the DeWolf ships' logs and ledgers that remain, any mention of the word "slaves" suddenly becomes glaringly absent.[286] With so many people from Rhode Island being involved for so long in the illegal trafficking of humans, it is curious that so many individuals believed that all illegal activity virtually stopped with the passing of yet another slave law. This is especially puzzling given the knowledge of DeWolf's political prowess and cunning ability to bypass previous laws in his continued pursuit of wealth and power. There remain multiple letters, both to and from DeWolf, that discuss the loosened standards of this powerful family regarding their neverending involvement in the slave trade.

On New Year's Day 1808, ships sailing for Africa virtually disappeared from the destination columns of customhouse records in Bristol. Additionally, nearly 80 to 90 percent of all voyages documented out of Bristol listed the Caribbean as their destination.[287] Concurrently, departures from Rhode Island to Cuba doubled in 1808. Cuba did not enact a slave trade law until it was forced to through diplomatic pressure by Spain in 1817. Yet it still remained illegal for an American citizen to participate in the slave trade domestically or abroad, despite the political standing in other countries.[288]

Ellery's prolific rate of correspondence continued in 1808 as he ineffectually attempted to stop DeWolf, and other Rhode Islanders, from breaking the law. Multiple letters were written in the month of March, which may have been the height of his frustration that year. During this time, Ellery referred to ships that declared on their manifests domestic destinations but in reality sailed directly to the foreign port of Havana, Cuba. In Ellery's correspondence, he reiterates slave trade laws that had been broken regarding customhouse violations, collections and different sections of laws from 1794 to 1808. Captains' names and names of vessels, most of which were owned by DeWolf, and which ports of call the vessels originated from in Rhode Island are all mentioned. The majority of these letters are written to David Howell or David Barnes, both in influential political positions and advisors to Ellery.[289]

Howell was a local Republican, and Barnes was appointed by President Jefferson as the United States attorney and, later, judge for the U.S. District Court of Rhode Island. Barnes was a fellow Republican and supporter of Jefferson. Both men were in powerful positions capable of supporting Ellery in the effort to end the illicit activity of DeWolf and others in the state. However, their presence was never fully felt by Ellery, nor did they have an impact on slowing the illegal activities in the port of Bristol.

DeWolf outwardly maintained the appearance of upholding the new law, his discretion demonstrated in the financial backing of his vessels and the removal of his name on the ships' manifests. His captains' names became more prevalent on the paperwork submitted to the customhouse. This was particularly vital, as families and local commerce depended heavily on DeWolf's active and continued success in the trade.

DeWolf owned a ship called the *Three Sisters*, which set sail from the port of Bristol on December 21, 1807. A successful journey to the coast of Africa, the first stop of the triangular trade route, could easily last six months. The *Three Sisters*'s destination was not listed, nor was its arrival date back to Bristol. But documented on the ship's log was that this voyage carried on board 117 slaves.[290] With ten days remaining in the month of December at the time of departure, there is no possibility that the *Three Sisters* could have departed from Bristol, picked up 117 slaves from Africa and then delivered them before January 1, 1808, the date the federal government outlawed participation in the international slave trade with its enhanced penalties.

Although regulations were stiffer, DeWolf vessels had no real obstacles that kept them from defrauding the laws. Reviewing the maritime activity of the three customhouses in Rhode Island from 1808 to 1812, the port of Bristol never lost its resilience, confirming that the mercantile community never abandoned its commitment to the slave trade.[291] Many residents of Bristol did not resist the temptation of garnering a substantial profit resulting from the trade, nor did they appear to be too concerned about a decline in social status, for their reputations as slavers seemed to bring them acclaim within the local community. In reality, slaving did not come to a complete stop but instead temporarily slowed during the War of 1812 and later resumed on an even larger scale once the war ended a short thirty-two months later.[292] The demand for slaves rose both domestically and internationally after the war, which concurrently drove up the price for slaves, as well as the profit margin for the DeWolfs.

Charles Clarke, a DeWolf crew member, wrote a letter to his mother on January 17, 1808, and surprisingly went into extraordinary detail about his arrival in Charleston, South Carolina, on January 14 with a load of slaves. He spoke of his arrival in port without any trouble and said that the slaves were being sold at that time for around $350 each. Clarke candidly explained that if "it had not been for this Embargo, they would been [*sic*] up to 500 dollars…I don't see that the trade stops much for they come in town 2 or 3 hundred some nights."[293] Clarke stated that they left the coast of Africa with seventy-one slaves and that four slaves died during the voyage. The letter left the impression that this was just another day in human trafficking and that the DeWolf crew member intended to stay in this business, regardless of the extra effort it took to deliver the slaves.

Clarke further explained, in detail, how the slaves were brought into Charleston now that the 1808 act had been implemented. He felt that at least five hundred slaves had already been delivered by the middle of January and that the slaves were delivered by landing the vessels outside the harbor, rowing them to shore and then marching them in at night. Two or three vessels a day would arrive from Africa, and one of the ways the ship's ballast was cleared by customs was to call the slaves "passengers." Clarke stated that another pattern that was commonly used was to have a vessel bound for New Orleans and then have it become "distressed," enabling it to sail directly to Havana to deliver its cargo. Clarke concluded his letter by stating that he had never seen so many vessels along the coastline of Charleston during winter before and that he believed there were at least two hundred belonging to the United States alone.[294]

By August 10, 1808, the Treasury Department sent a letter to Collector Collins regarding a vessel that was registered in Bristol and its attempt to offload its cargo in Charleston. The letter declared that the ship's manifest showed inaccuracies; it stated that the ship carried on board many items that were either illegal or undeclared, and the crew had knowledge of the offense. It also cited the reloading of illegal materials affiliated with the slave trade onto the ship and noted that the ship had prepared to leave unlawfully for the West Indies.[295] While there is not direct mention of this vessel belonging to DeWolf, he had faced such allegations before regarding many of his vessels. Collins's response to such accusations as the collector was to ignore both Ellery and the Department of Treasury while protecting his friend and brother-in-law, as well as his personal financial bottom line.

Collins was bound by federal regulation to abide by the same laws as the owners, captains and crew members of all vessels that freely participated in the slave trade. The relentless illegal activity in Bristol's port made Collins just as guilty as DeWolf regarding the defiance of the laws; if convicted, violators could be punished by death.

Over time, Ellery began to receive letters from community members who were beginning to complain about the illegal activity surrounding Bristol Harbor. On October 23, 1808, the surveyor of Warren, a port neighboring Bristol and in the same jurisdiction wrote a letter to both Collins and Ellery requesting that they take action against a vessel. The surveyor stated that he believed the vessel was preparing to leave port without being legally bonded.[296] Outfitting vessels for the slave trade with restraint implements and other hardware specific to the slave trade was all that was needed to impound a vessel and arrest the crew. It was not necessary to actually see slaves. As a result of the contraband items on board, many ships would bypass the inspection that would entitle them to be bonded to sail. It was this procedure that gave the declaration that would prove the vessel abided by the law. Collins, who most assuredly had no intention of taking legal action against the vessel, often left letters unanswered, which would have added to Ellery's incessant frustration.

On November 10, 1808, Ellery wrote to Collins and declared that there was yet another vessel that had taken in goods without the inspection of the proper revenue officers and reminded him to identify any future vessels, in similar circumstances, and impound them.[297] With the knowledge that Collins freely falsified customhouse records, it is highly probable that he was keenly aware of most of these incidents. Collins continued to assist traders in illegally transporting human cargo once they departed from Rhode Island, a pattern that reliably continued to benefit DeWolf and his family.

In December 1808, Ellery vainly attempted, once again, to send correspondence to Collins that informed the Bristol collector that he was aware of plans forming in his port in contravention of the embargo laws. Ellery further discussed in the letter the seemingly great difficulty it would be for Collins to prevent this from happening as a result of his austere approach in upholding the law. A specific vessel was mentioned in the letter, and Ellery noted that it had left Bristol and exited Narragansett Bay around sunset. Attempts to stop the vessel were made by a gunboat issuing warning shots, but it did not yield, sailing toward the open sea under prevailing winds.[298] Understandably, there would be no reason for a vessel to run from a gunboat as the sun set unless it was outfitted with equipment for the sole reason of purchasing and transporting slaves. DeWolf owned ships that were of the latest modernization and were well known to have the ability to outrun the standard vessel of the day, particularly those provided by the federal government.

These few letters exhibit a disturbing pattern with regards to vessels involved in illegal activities leaving the port of Bristol, which included many DeWolf ships that only a collector could have allowed. It appeared at first that there were just a few random vessels attempting one final, yet illegal, voyage. However, correspondence to Collector Collins indicated that this pattern did not end anytime soon. Numerous letters written by Ellery, sent not only to Collins but also to the Treasury Department, addressed the continuance of these infractions of the law, all based at the port of Bristol.[299] There was the continued use of foreign flags, already established as common practice, on American vessels in an effort to circumvent the law. However, the act had been interpreted correctly in that no clearance should be granted from an American port if bonds were not presented, regardless of their international affiliation or purpose of their departure. Issuing a bond to a vessel was the proof the captain needed to show intent of a legal voyage. Pointing out the temptations to evade the laws, newspaper commentaries were published requesting that, under the existing circumstances, the public should challenge the port collector to reassess Collins's performance of his official duties.

Not until President Jefferson's successor, James Madison, was sworn into office on March 4, 1809, was the topic of illegal trafficking of humans once again formally addressed. Madison declared on record that nothing could exceed the wickedness and folly that continued to rule in Rhode Island and that all sense of character had been obliterated.[300]

Unfortunately for Ellery, just one month later, an article appeared in the local newspaper with some distressing news. As acting secretary of the treasury, Gallatan was acutely aware of the illegal activities that prevailed at Bristol's port. Gallatan wrote a commentary that was placed in the *Bristol County Register* on April 8, 1809. It specifically addressed the legality of foreign vessels in the port of Bristol under the law of 1808. Gallatan stated that the embargo laws were so blatantly ignored in Rhode Island that he felt it was unnecessary to continue the extraordinary expense that had been authorized for the sole purpose of enforcement. He then declared that all of the authorities given to employ additional boats, officers or men for that purpose must be considered revoked. This news would have been enthusiastically received by DeWolf and his brothers but profoundly distressing to Ellery. The federal government had just publicly declared defeat, leaving Ellery alone and without support—again.[301]

By 1810, two years after the ratification of the slave law that was allegedly designed to end slave trading once and for all, Madison renewed his warning to Congress, stating that American citizens were instrumental in carrying on traffic in enslaved Africans. He further declared that American citizens were equally in violation of the laws of humanity and in defiance of those of their own country.[302] Madison admonished that the slave trade had become so notorious in the United States that, in 1810, he informed Congress that it was necessary to readdress improvement on existing legislation. However, funding for the purpose of enforcement of the law was not addressed. The Act of 1808 that was intended to end the importation of enslaved people by American citizens had little impact. Two new revisions to the 1808 act were written but not passed until 1818. The first revision gave half of the fines collected to informers, and in 1820, the second revision stated that if a captain, owner or crew member was found guilty in a trial, it was punishable by death.[303] The unfortunate reality is that it took Congress another twelve years to pass these two, more powerful revisions to the act, which openly divulges the opinion of the majority of our congressional leaders at the time.

In January 1811, the U.S. secretary of the navy, Paul Hamilton, wrote to the naval commander at Charleston: "I hear, not without great concern, that the law prohibiting the importation of slaves has been violated in frequent instances."[304] Hamilton was keenly aware of the overwhelming responsibility placed on the U.S. Navy to enforce slave trade laws. With multiple national obligations and an insufficient fleet, his clearly articulated comment was repleet with frustration. It also confirmed, once again, the negated enforcement put into place by Congress, supporting Ellery's primary complaint.

Unfortunately for abolitionists everywhere, the United States had one of the largest loopholes imaginable regarding the trade. Spain still maintained ownership of the Florida Territory, which happened to be in the Spanish-controlled backyard of Cuba. It was convenient for American slavers to smuggle slaves from the Caribbean or Cuba through Florida and eventually into the southern states. It was also the territory to which slaves from the South escaped and ultimately where many were captured and then resold.

The United States did not acquire Florida as a territory until 1822, which helped cultivate the downfall of the slave trade onboard American vessels as a result of its proximity to Cuba.[305] This was a brilliant opportunity for American slavers to capitalize on their acquisition of Cuban sugar plantations, holding slaves on their estates while prices were low in Havana and creating a convenient staging site for smuggling slaves into the United States.[306]

By 1812, President Madison had acquired abundant information to once again address Congress about the blatant disregard American slavers had for the law. The president amassed suitable evidence to discuss multiple vessels that passed illegally, without interruption, in and out of U.S. ports and which had no part in the War of 1812. Unsurprisingly, two of DeWolf's vessels were discussed as an example of illegal activity. As always, DeWolf's vessels were illegally permitted to pass inspection, under the supervision of Collector Collins. These incidents were most notably documented as such in the congressional record of July 7 and July 9, 1812.[307]

Retaining his position of power for twenty years, Collins freely permitted owners to change their ships' registries at will, as they only needed to be filed locally. Collins repeatedly received correspondence from many individuals, Ellery included, who challenged him to uphold the laws. As long as Collins stayed in the position of collector and remained connected to the slave trade, DeWolf and the town of Bristol remained intimately connected to the trade. In the meantime, Ellery independently endeavored to fulfill his responsibility of upholding the law.[308]

On October 4, 1813, a cryptic letter was written to John DeWolf that was to be discussed with James. It was sent by John W. Rufus, who was in

Havana at the time. Within the correspondence, Rufus explained that the proceeds of a "certain shipment mentioned there in [*sic*]" would be divided equally into four parts and that the shipment was solely in the DeWolf name to simplify business. Rufus went on to explain that the vessel left on the date of the letter and was headed to an "unblocked port in the Northern part of the U.S." Additionally, he warned, the risk of the vessel landing was to be considered equal to all who are financially vested in the shipment. He closed the letter declaring that it was difficult to discuss things during that time, as business could not safely be explained on paper.[309]

A pattern of defiance for the law and the creative nature that was used to avoid it continued to expand. One such example of this can be seen when an American owner or owners of a vessel falsified a bill of sale for their ship, allegedly signing it over to a foreigner. The new foreign captain was always from a country that had yet to outlaw the trade, typically Spain, and would be given money to purchase a cargo of slaves. Before the vessel sailed, the new foreign owner would reconvey the vessel and declaration of all future cargo back to the former American owner(s), for a price, and the American owner(s) would gain the profits from the sale of slaves when the vessel returned. DeWolf perfected this process when he hired Spanish captains and then forged the records, allowing him to continue in the trade.[310]

By December 1815, Ellery's letter-writing campaign had reached new heights. He wrote to Collins and stated that vessels continued to fit out under Spanish colors and depart from the port of Bristol. Most specifically, Ellery referred to a vessel, the *Macdonough*, which he knew to be owned by DeWolf. Ellery explained to Collins how such a sale to a Spaniard occurred and how it would have enabled DeWolf tremendously. Ellery knew that Collins was aware of this fact but tirelessly wrote to him regarding the continual infractions of the law in and out of the port of Bristol. The assumption made by Ellery regarding the *Macdonough* was actually correct; it was a DeWolf vessel owned by nephew George, with his uncle James as an investor. The American captain for this vessel was Oliver James Wilson, but the acting Spanish master of the vessel on record was Joseph Dolores Herrero.[311]

Ellery stated that a crew member from the *Macdonough* came into port and secretly reported to Ellery the infractions that the vessel had committed. The man stated that the vessel was outfitted as a slave carrier with handcuffs and fetters, concealed in casks, for the purpose of binding slaves to prevent insurrection. The crewman then declared that it would soon sail for the coast of Africa with the sole intention of purchasing slaves. It would then carry its cargo to a port in the West Indies for sale.[312]

A watercolor of the *Macdonough* by Jonathan Alger Jr. The vessel was captained by General George DeWolf and owned with his uncle James DeWolf as a silent partner. *Photo taken by author, with permission from the Bristol Historical and Preservation Society.*

Ellery immediately took action and asked the local surveyor, Mr. Slocum, to go on board the *Macdonough* early the following morning to obtain papers of compliance and ownership. Ellery wanted to confirm whether it was Spanish and whether the vessel was in violation of the Act of 1808. Unfortunately, the vessel had left late the prior evening, even though it was a cloudy night with limited visibility and the winds were blowing southward against the brig's departure. The vessel struggled through the early morning hours in Narragansett Bay to make its way to the open sea. When Slocum discovered its departure, he immediately sent for the revenue boat to pick him up and attempt to intercept the runaway vessel. Once the *Macdonough* passed the inner harbor, the boat had all sails in full hail, but the revenue boat managed to catch up to it and successfully communicate with Wilson on board. Slocum asked Wilson if he might be able to come on board. Wilson replied that he could, but the passage that they were presently in was too narrow and he needed to sail a little farther on to find a more desirable location. This was, unfortunately for Slocum, a bold delay tactic. As the *Macdonough* came closer to the open sea, it was suddenly able to outrun the revenue boat, which eventually had to give up, turn around and return to port unsuccessful.[313]

When Ellery asked Slocum to have a conversation about this incident with the collector, Collins boldly responded to Slocum's questioning by defiantly insisting that there were three or four vessels that had recently departed from the port of Bristol for the same reason and had arrived at Havana with more than two hundred slaves. Collins than recklessly stated that since there was no complaint filed by anyone, he did not feel it was necessary to take a bond for the vessels or a manifest with the crew members' names.[314]

Collins then feigned sorrow that such an unlawful trade should be carried on and stated that he would let his brother-in-law know of the situation regarding the *Macdonough*. Clearly, Collins's statement was meant to pacify Ellery, as Collins was a devout DeWolf ally and knew that DeWolf would be happy with the information of the vessel's safe departure. Ellery's letter to Collins closed with a final plea that stated that unless some more efficacious means were devised and used to put a stop to the illegal traffic, it would continue to increase, for it remained very lucrative financially for all involved.[315] Ellery could not have stated the financial motivation for the slave trade more clearly. DeWolf not only financially backed the *Macdonough*, but he also insured it through his company Mount Hope Insurance. The *Macdonough* did in fact acquire approximately three hundred slaves. Its final destination was Cuba, not the West Indies, where it ran aground on a shallow reef.[316]

On January 6, 1816, DeWolf was on a voyage—the journey on the *Andromache* was not his last—and he wrote a letter to his brother John using coordinates at sea at the time of his writing. He was fourteen days out from the coast of Africa and presumably mailed the letter from the West Indies, as he concluded that he was five or six days away from his arrival in Havana. The letter is very telling, as he discussed the difficult winds that were against him through the Middle Passage and claimed they had severely delayed his trip. Not only does this letter substantiate his continuance in the trade, but it also confirms that he was still a hands-on captain.

In typical business fashion, DeWolf discussed ongoing projects that he had in Baltimore, New York and Philadelphia, including different captains' names, cargo and destinations of delivery. DeWolf closed his letter showing concern for his wife, asking John to tell her that he was safe.[317] Looking back to previously written historical accounts, it becomes clear that DeWolf never went on a farewell voyage but professedly sailed to give the impression that he was finally done with the trade. Certainly, he was hoping that the attention he had so readily received leading up to 1808 would be diverted elsewhere.

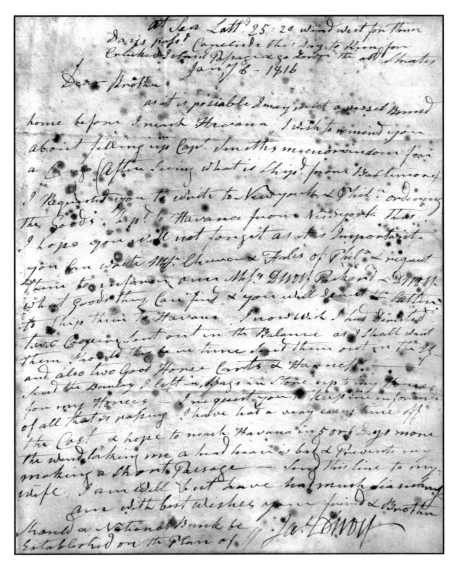

DeWolf using latitude and longitude coordinates at sea. DeWolf family letters allowed for accurate interpretation of where vessels traveled to, despite what was reported to the customhouse. *Photo taken by author, with permission from the Bristol Historical and Preservation Society.*

Less than two months later, on February 1, 1816, Ellery sent a letter to Collins that pleaded for him to stop the continuance of illegal activity out of Bristol. Well into his elder years, Ellery stayed committed to his federally appointed position as Rhode Island collector. He became acutely aware of three additional vessels that departed from Bristol with the sole intention of buying slaves, specifically to be sold at a foreign port. Of the three vessels, Ellery concluded that at least one of them belonged to James DeWolf. Outlining in tremendous detail the ships' names, captains, destinations and the fact that they, too, sailed under Spanish colors, Ellery made what appeared to be one last appeal to Collins, requesting his help to bring an end to the illegal activity in his port.[318]

In his letter, Ellery stated that it was Collins's duty to detect all who were involved in the slave trade and to inflict the law and all of its penalties on those who transgressed. He further reminded Collins that he was responsible for giving him the information about the vessels that had violated the law and any other information he had the power to obtain that would be helpful in stopping the slave trade in Bristol.[319] Ellery's letter books are replete with correspondence documenting DeWolf and other Rhode Island captains and their illegal exploits. The frustration that Ellery must have felt over the years of having to contend with DeWolf, and then Collins, clearly seemed to consume him, as evidenced by his pattern of correspondence. However, despite Ellery's concerted efforts, the slaving activity never truly slowed in Bristol, at least not where the DeWolfs were concerned.

Bristolian legend claimed that Collins left his position as collector on his own accord and that the customhouse logs could not be located after his departure. It was stated that he burned all of the records, including correspondence, dating from 1804 until 1820.[320] It was believed that Collins destroyed the information in an effort to protect not only himself but also the rest of the DeWolf family from prosecution as a result of breaking so many state and federal laws.[321] Much of this information came from George Howe's family memoir, a colorful and descriptive rendition of the DeWolfs' lives in Bristol. Unfortunately, many historians have relied too heavily on his narrative as historical fact. With the collection of DeWolf correspondence, ledgers and ships' logs from multiple archived sources, it becomes increasingly clear that while the skeleton of Howe's story is fairly accurate, there are many details that have been embellished to create a more interesting tale. Perhaps it was also written in this manner to dissuade future DeWolf generations from knowing the truth. As it stood, DeWolf remained quite vested in the trade, both financially and definitively, for years after his well-known farewell voyage on the *Andromache*.

Chapter 10

SLAVES AND CUBA

Purchase for me...half male and half female young negros [sic], *but not small ones.*[322]
—*James DeWolf, 1817*

I n 1817, Spain signed a treaty to abolish the slave trade in all of its territories, including Cuba. In this treaty, it was written that the Spanish navy could seize any ship believed to be involved in illegally trading slaves. This not only included captains and vessels but also the masters and owners of slaves. Later, the treaty was amended to exclude Portugal and the Netherlands, stating that those two countries could continue to trade slaves in Spanish territories provided they were south of the Equator. However, the treaty purposely did not prevent the United States or France from trading or owning slaves in Spanish territories. It was not uncommon for a Spanish or Dutch ship to sale under a U.S. or French flag, reversing the same process used by American vessels.[323]

Taking complete advantage of this coveted loophole, DeWolf wrote a letter on January 25, 1817, to one of his many captains, John Smith. In his correspondence, he discussed sugar and coffee transfers from his Cuban plantations but boldly, or carelessly, stated an additional request. DeWolf included in his letter:

> *I want a few negros* [sic] *for each of my plantations, say ten for each* [thirty total] *which I wish you could purchase for me from same cargo which may arrive half male and half female young negros* [sic], *but no*

small ones.[324]

Continuing to participate in the slave trade, DeWolf allowed the recipient of that letter to understand what his undeniable request was without the worry of deciphering hidden messages or code. There remained no obvious compulsion to adhere to the Act of 1808, ending all assumptions that he was no longer involved in the business of trafficking humans.

DeWolf wrote multiple letters in 1817 that outlined the various captains he employed, the names of their vessels and continual instructions and references to cargo. Each vessel's final destination was Cuba; many dropped their cargo not only in Havana but in Matanzas as well. Included in a letter dated October 7, 1817, were explicit instructions to drop the cargo in Matanzas, where DeWolf owned a plantation maintained by hundreds of slaves.[325] Having a plantation in this Cuban location was an interesting choice, as the protected harbor of Matanzas Bay is quite similar for unloading cargo to Bristol Harbor in Narragansett Bay. The docking point for DeWolf's vessels in Matanzas were on the right side of the bay as you entered from the open ocean, the same as Bristol Harbor. The similarities were uncanny. The only difference was that DeWolf had his own facility for loading and unloading cargo in Bristol. In Matanzas, the unloading and holding area for slaves was a fort at the water's edge that coincidentally was built by slaves. DeWolf, at this time, also maintained his active and visible role as a politician and member of the Rhode Island House of Representatives.

DeWolf loyally employed family, extended family and community members, some becoming so financially dependent on DeWolf's success that they would turn a blind eye to his illegal activities. Among his faithful family members who worked for him were his in-laws, the Bradfords. Captain William Bradford, the son of Senator Bradford and DeWolf's brother-in-law, received a letter from DeWolf written on October 27, 1817. DeWolf acknowledged the agreement that was made with the younger Bradford to sail on DeWolf's brig *Remitance* to the coastal town of Trinidad, Cuba. While there is no distinct or obvious reference to slaves on this voyage, DeWolf referred to cargo that would be received by a Mr. Baker once he arrived in Trinidad. Once the cargo was sold, Bradford would then receive sugar to bring back to Bristol.[326]

There were many working sugar plantations in Trinidad, as well as throughout Cuba, during this time that maintained a high demand for slaves. DeWolf requested that Bradford should not only sell the contents of the vessel but the vessel as well. This would eliminate any question of

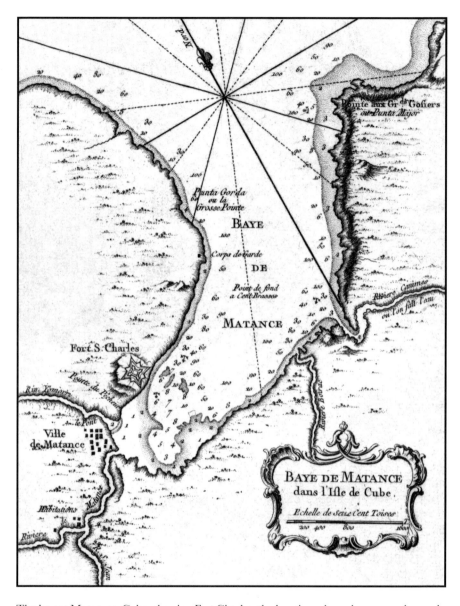

The bay at Matanzas, Cuba, showing Fort Charles, the location where slaves were dropped off. Created by Jacques Nicolas Bellin in 1764. *Courtesy of the Library of Congress, digital call number 73697700.*

whether it had been fitted out for illegal trade once it returned to Bristol, confirming that there was an exchange of slaves for sugar. Bradford was further instructed to take the proceeds from the sale and purchase

Fort Charles at Matanzas Bay, known today as San Severino Castle, had damp, dark cells that had remnants of restraint apparatus. The fort was built by slaves. *Photo taken by author.*

a smaller vessel, load it with the sugar and sail back to Rhode Island. DeWolf then advised Bradford to make Boston his port of destination on his manifest, adding that if the wind should be in his favor, DeWolf preferred that he sail to the port of New York since the demand for sugar there would result in a higher profit.[327]

With a new sitting president came renewed recognition of the continued infractions made by U.S. citizens in regards to the 1808 act. Introduced by President Monroe and passed by Congress were some strengthened revisions to the law. Henry Clay, Speaker of the House, and John Gaillard, president of the Senate pro tempore, once again put a ban on importing slaves, required the forfeiture of ships built for such a purpose and increased the penalties for involvement in the slave trade. Essentially, the revision to the Act of 1808 read nearly identical to its original, only this time it included heightened penalties and fines if caught participating in the slave trade.[328] Unfortunately, Spanish-controlled Cuba did everything in its power to allow the trade to continue, particularly for Americans.

Its policy of protecting the vessels that traveled to and from its ports was well known not only to U.S. captains but also to others because it brought tremendous cash flow to the island.[329]

Ellery's letter campaign showed a lull at this point, but the illegal activity of slave trading in his state did not. By 1818, Barnabas Bates, Bristol's postmaster, had written a letter of complaint to Ellery stating that, in his observation, the system of buying and selling slaves had been perfected in Bristol. He stated that vessels that departed from that port were usually suited for the African market. He further stated that the vessels were always cleared by collector Collins for Havana as their final destination. He stated the obvious—that once these vessels suited for the illegal trade arrived in Africa, slaves were taken aboard and then sailed directly to Cuba. Bates ended his formal complaint by stating that most of the vessels he was referring to were owned or partially owned by DeWolf.[330]

Continuing to generate a copious pattern of slave delivery, DeWolf again touched base with his brothers in Bristol. Corresponding from Havana in March 1818, DeWolf wrote an atypically long letter discussing business but also referencing Spain's Treaty of 1817. DeWolf spoke of the Spanish government entertaining the idea of stopping the importation of Negroes altogether, which would have an impact on both the United States and France, and it was enticing him to purchase some additional slaves. But to do this, DeWolf added, he needed some extra cash. He then inquired if the Bank of Bristol, his personal bank, could help him with a loan and said that he would gladly embrace its assistance.[331]

As collector, Charles Collins was not only a supportive ally in port but also helped DeWolf manage the family businesses in Cuba, including the transaction of slaves. In February 1819, Collins was on a trip to one of DeWolf's coffee plantation investments located in Matanzas. Once he arrived, Collins wrote an urgent letter to DeWolf to discuss the business of coffee that was to be shipped to Bristol. Subsequently, he went into a lengthy and detailed report regarding the slaves on the plantation. He began by repeating a quote that DeWolf had previously stated to Collins about the care he must have over the horses and slaves on the estate and that he would prefer a level of discretion by not allowing too many visitors.[332]

The letter then transitioned when Collins made a bold business statement to DeWolf about the unfortunate situation of slaves who were stolen from the Matanzas location. Collins stated there was not anything that could be done about the stolen slaves or about the money that was due for them now that they were gone. The letter expanded by confirming that the slaves who were missing were initially the ones designated to be sold for profit on DeWolf's behalf. Collins then asked DeWolf to manage this situation, suggesting that DeWolf repurchase twenty slaves, female only, to replace those who were stolen.[333] Always maintaining observant alertness in his economic environment can perhaps explain why so many of the slave purchases toward the conclusion of DeWolf's career were young women entering childbearing age. The purchase of additional slaves in 1819 by a United States citizen did not appear to be of any concern to either Collins or DeWolf.

One of the reasons DeWolf remained successful in the illegal transport of slaves well past 1808 was that he maintained a position in Rhode Island politics for nearly the remainder of his life. To have a seat in a decision-making assembly greatly enhanced DeWolf's ability to persuade committee members toward his opinion and to understand the value of regulations of new and old laws. In particular, this one factor allowed DeWolf the opportunity to continue his creative circumvention of the laws without prosecution, empowering him to sustain his extensive business plan.

Another factor that would have aided in DeWolf's continuance of the trade was the death of his law-abiding nemesis. William Ellery died in February, 1820 at the age of ninety-two, while still holding the office of Rhode Island's head collector.[334] Ellery was ultimately replaced by his nephew, former senator Christopher Ellery, who was responsible for helping the Rhode Island contingency speak to Jefferson about appointing Collins as collector in Bristol. Christopher Ellery remained as the custom collector of Newport for fourteen years, retiring in 1834.[335] Just when it seemed like DeWolf's prolific pattern of trade would continue with ease, President James Monroe declined to reappoint Collins as collector of Bristol, and he was permanently removed. However, at the age of forty-seven, Charles Collins could not be dissuaded from continuing to support his family and decided to pursue his own political career locally.[336]

The same year Ellery died and Collins was replaced, DeWolf ran for office in Congress. After running a successful campaign, DeWolf was sworn in as a U.S. senator on March 4, 1821, representing his home state of Rhode Island. During his incredibly short senatorial tenure, DeWolf was credited with leading Congress in a very influential and successful fight against proposed legislation in 1823 that attempted, once again, to strengthen slave-trading laws within our nation. As a result of DeWolf's leadership in the Senate, this proposed law was

A political circular (1819) discussing the opposing political party and its attempts to dethrone the Republicans. A copy was sent to DeWolf and Collins to circulate throughout Bristol. *Photo taken by author, with permission from the Bristol Historical and Preservation Society.*

tragically defeated, removing it from further discussion indefinitely.[337]

Throughout DeWolf's correspondence, multiple letters can be seen where he was beginning to manage his plantations in Cuba more frequently from Bristol. On October 15, 1821, DeWolf wrote of the loss of a vessel to pirates that ultimately created a financial debt for one of his coffee estates. DeWolf sent money in his letter to get the estate out of arrears so he would not be financially indebted to anyone. Once the monetary matter was outlined, the discussion returned to the matter of a shipment of coffee that still needed to be sent to Bristol.[338]

Continuing to have a working relationship with his brother-in-law, Collins sent a letter to Senator DeWolf regarding the slaves on one of DeWolf's Cuban estates. The letter, dated October 19, 1823, stated that Collins had just spoken with one of DeWolf's captains, who had just returned to port. The captain reported that there was a substantial increase in the slave population on DeWolf's estate. What is not clear is whether the increase was due to the delivery of additional slaves or whether babies were being born to slaves. Reproduction of slaves was strongly encouraged, as it was not only safer than circumventing international slave laws but also much less costly to the owner. New births were most likely the scenario when the number of recent female slave purchases is taken into consideration. Interestingly, a short time after Collins wrote this letter, he was sworn in as the new lieutenant governor of Rhode Island in 1824 and remained in this position until 1833.[339]

Although DeWolf owned his slaves in a territory that originally permitted the enslavement of Africans, the Federal Slave Trade Act of 1808 had not changed its stance on the legality of Americans' involvement and participation in such activities. While still a sitting senator, DeWolf received a letter from Havana dated February 16, 1824. The envelope was addressed to the "Hon. James DeWolf, Senator in Congress, Washington D.C." Joel Abbot, author of the letter and a DeWolf captain, had just arrived in Havana after an unsuccessful attempt to drop his cargo of slaves in Matanzas, intended for DeWolf's plantation, and to pick up a new load of sugar. He stated that sailing away from Africa and then through the Middle Passage was rough, as the wind continued to be very strong. As a result, he needed to sail north and then west toward the more protected harbor of Havana. After he discussed his decision of landing at a secondary port, Abbott further stated that DeWolf's choice of vessel, of which he had given him charge, sailed well, as there were pirates who were actively capturing or robbing vessels. However, at this point, because of the speed and stability of the ship, he, the cargo and his crew were fine.[340]

DeWolf surprisingly resigned early from the Senate on October 31, 1825, before the completion of his first term. Family lore claimed that DeWolf left the congressional position early because of his growing distrust of President John Q. Adams and the president's political ideals.

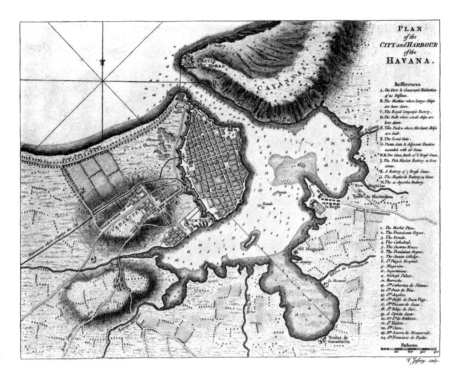

Map of Havana Harbor and its city, created by Thomas Jefferys, 1768. *Courtesy of Library of Congress, digital call number 74690536.*

It is also said that he wanted to return to Bristol to keep an eye on his slaving nephew George, who had become quite careless as a business partner, taking too many unnecessary risks.[341] No correspondence written by DeWolf has been found that has revealed his true reason for leaving the Senate before his term expired, but if his decision was based on protecting the family fortune, it would stand to reason. Once DeWolf returned to Bristol, he set his sights, once again, on holding a local political position in Rhode Island. He ran a successful campaign and returned to his previous post in the state House of Representatives from 1829 until the day he unexpectedly died in 1837.[342]

While positioning to run for a local office, and one year after his resignation from Congress, there was a sudden mortality of slaves in September 1826 on one of DeWolf's plantations. It was most likely due to a local cholera epidemic that had just begun.[343] DeWolf wrote a lengthy letter of discussion to Captain Bradford concerning the loss of life and then asked that Bradford try to do something about squelching

Cuban Estate Arc de Noé (Noah's Ark), artist and year unknown. *Photo taken by author with permission from Linden Place.*

the illness and the need to repurchase a replacement of slaves. There was a brief moment in the letter that could be interpreted as DeWolf showing compassion or concern regarding the loss of life that was hitting his slave population so hard. However, the letter then continued, in lengthy detail, about the business of selling coffee at the right market price, the crop itself and the future of the next harvest. It was clear with these concluding comments that he was thinking of his financial bottom line and how costly it would be to replace his captive laborers.[344]

DeWolf corresponded with Bradford the following month, in October, but this time to complain about the next generation of DeWolfs. He was particularly concerned about his nephew George and his inability to handle money correctly. DeWolf then cautioned Bradford to be wary of all the cousins and their ability to borrow money or their failure to fulfill their current obligations within the family empire. Finally DeWolf stated that he, at the age of sixty-two, would travel to Cuba the following month and hoped to find things in good order regarding the slaves and the young coffee plants.[345]

By 1828, DeWolf had directed his sons in a more active role regarding his plantations, primarily because of his age. On December 15, Mark

Anthony DeWolf, son of James, wrote to Bradford stating that his father wanted him to travel to Cuba to the Mariana coffee estate just east of Havana. The sole purpose of the trip was to assess how the plantation had recently been managed. Mark Anthony expressed that he was certain that the Mariana had been taken care of, even before his arrival, particularly because he felt that Bradford had a positive disposition while he governed the slaves. Bradford had the desirable trait of an administrator to maintain control over the workers.[346]

Captain Bradford continued to work for DeWolf in Cuba, which can be verified with a letter from Havana dated April 4, 1829. Included in this letter was documentation of an itemization of services and property rendered. One line showed that Bradford rented seventy slaves for twenty days on DeWolf's behalf to the estate of Dr. Morel at the cost of $600. This money was then credited to DeWolf's Cuban estate while he was a political representative to the House in Rhode Island.[347]

Ever present, Collins sent a letter to DeWolf on December 10, 1829, and recommended that a gentleman by the name of John Anderson be hired to work as a cook on one of DeWolf's vessels. He spoke of the reputation and sobriety of Anderson and said that Collins, lieutenant governor of Rhode Island, had no doubt that Anderson would maintain a high level of discretion and be a good fit on one of DeWolf's crews.[348] This correspondence further confirmed that DeWolf still owned a large and active fleet of vessels, even in 1829, and found it necessary to take great care in the hiring of discerning crew members. There is plenty of documentation confirming that DeWolf had a large fleet used for transportation and trade. The notion that he needed to continue to hire individuals who were discreet would not have been necessary if all of his business transactions were of a legal nature.

As the years passed, the letters were much of the same, discussing the business of the Cuban estates. The correspondence would outline the status of the slaves, coffee plants and the buying and selling of both coffee and sugar. By 1833, DeWolf was attempting to sell his portion of an investment in a Cuban coffee estate named the Empresa. DeWolf was financially vested for a total of one-third of this particular plantation and no longer wanted to be a partner. His board of directors from the Bank of Bristol advised him that an arrangement could be made to remove one-third of the slaves from the estate and sell them separately from the sale of the property. The board then determined that the sale of the slaves alone would bring a financial profit for DeWolf valued at half of all the land, buildings and remaining slaves on the estate. This would be a far more desirable alternative, financially, than to sell his investment as an inclusive package. Unfortunately for the slaves, it would have included the tearing apart of existing family units within the estate, something that was clearly of no concern to DeWolf.[349]

Epilogue

THE DEMISE OF A SLAVE TRADER

In 1829, DeWolf reestablished his position in the House of Representatives in Rhode Island with the intention of exerting political influence that would benefit his business enterprises. He most certainly could not have imagined that his life would end a mere eight years later. While conducting business and subsequently visiting his daughter in New York, DeWolf unexpectedly died on December 21, 1837, at the age of seventy-three. When his wife, Ann, received news of her husband's demise, Bristolian legend states that she promptly sequestered herself to her room, grief-stricken. She apparently refused to leave her confines, and twelve days after her husband's death, on January 2, 1838, she died as well.

In a memorial sermon delivered by Bishop Alexander V. Griswold on February 11, 1838, in Bristol, Rhode Island, both James's and Ann DeWolf's lives were honored.[350] The lengthy, scripture-filled tribute reviewed the career path of DeWolf and declared that he had been misled by his mother and slaving father, "their intentions [*sic*] ever so good, they know not always what is best for their children."[351] After Bishop Griswold justified DeWolf's career choice, he later honored him as a good husband and father, illustrating that his parenting skills were evident and neglecting to mention that his children followed him into the family business.[352] The most telling part of the fourteen-page dissertation stated:

> *Considering the rank which the head of this family had long sustained among you; his influence in society; the deep and active interest which he has*

taken in whatever concerned the public good; the great numbers of people that he has employed in useful labour [sic], and furnished with the means of living; the large share he has contributed to the wealth and prosperity of this town, and other public good, of which he has been the instrument, together with the extensive family connexions [sic] who yet survive to mourn his loss—when all these and other like considerations are brought into view, I may well address this congregation generally in the language of sympathy, as having lost a father—a public benefactor.[353]

As Bishop Griswold brought the DeWolfs' tribute to a close, he stated to the congregation that DeWolf's "industry was blest [sic] in the accumulation of ample fortune, which has benefitted not his family only, but many others."[354] Seemingly, while honoring the slaver's memory, Bishop Griswold suggested that the congregation forgive DeWolf for his choice of profession while acknowledging that his industry, and the town of Bristol, benefitted greatly as a whole.[355]

Disclosed in DeWolf's last will and testament was an inordinate amount of wealth that he was able to acquire during his lifetime as a slave trader. Within the document are numerous buildings, homes and farms and thousands of acres of land within the states of Rhode Island, Kentucky, Ohio, New York and Maryland. There was also the ownership of Hog Island, just across the bay from the port of Bristol; three manufacturing companies; and 1,686 shares in the Blackstone Canal Company. DeWolf owned 50 percent of two Cuban plantations, one coffee and one sugar, and a third plantation outright. The wharf estate that DeWolf so meticulously built with his brothers ended up solely in his name. It included the water lot, bank buildings, stores, the warehouse and more. He owned numerous vessels, both large and small, and all of the sails and riggings required for them to properly function. Finally, the bank holdings and liquid cash that DeWolf bequeathed to his family added up to thousands of dollars, equivalent to millions by twenty-first-century standards.

A generous provision was left by DeWolf for his wife, Ann, who did not live long enough to truly understand his generosity. She received their family home, the Mount, and its thirty acres of land; all provisions in the house, including all horses and carriages; Fox Hill with twenty-eight acres; and $3,000 annually from Bank of Bristol stock dividends, valued at $60,000. The remaining properties, stock holdings and cash were divided among his eight surviving children and four grandchildren. Little is known about what happened to Ann's inheritance. She had previously stated to her family that she would like her personal holdings be given to the school in Bristol. One can only assume that her desire was fulfilled and that the remaining acquisitions and properties were peacefully divided among her surviving children.

With the presumption of DeWolf harboring a fondness for his personal slaves, ultimately referred to as his servants, it was a bit disappointing to find that he made no provisions for them in his will. It might have been assumed that they would stay with Mrs. DeWolf and remain together in their elder years, but upon her death merely two weeks after her husband, Adjua and Pauledore found themselves suddenly unemployed.

Throughout history, the North has been seen as the liberator of enslaved people and the South as the oppressor. However, their true similarities become apparent through the scrutiny of economics. Both the North and South benefitted financially from the slave trade at the expense of the African race. The obvious shift in attitude toward slavery showed a quicker transition in the North, with a large contingency of abolitionists and their effort toward exposing the perversion of the trade. With the advancement of the abolition movement creating more visibility, slaves transitioned from property to humans. When this shift finally happened, people either agreed with this reality or bred a policy of racial discrimination. These ideas transcended through both the North and the South, but the North is credited with initiating the move toward the humanization of chattel.

So what side was DeWolf on? He shared elements of both regions and perhaps was conflicted by his career choice. DeWolf seemed to show compassion for his personal slaves but treated the thousands of others he transported as purely business. He became a leader in the slave trade industry, staying one step ahead of both reformers and the law, which would suggest that it was simply about money.

DeWolf was a compelling man when he was alive. He presented a persona that provoked a love-hate relationship with those around him. It also begged the question of whether he was a genius entrepreneur or a cutthroat businessman. At the end of his life, did DeWolf became reflective toward what he had accomplished, legal or not? Was there ever any remorse for the actions he took to build his successful empire at the expense of so many human lives? Was he ever tired of running, hiding, bribing or manipulating the truth? How did he see his legacy? With the exception of doubting that his sons and nephews had the ability or drive to carry on the family business, which happened to be true, no family letters have surfaced that would shed light on any of these questions.

Through the transition of multiple laws and numerous presidential administrations, James DeWolf remained a powerful and influential figure, both politically and as a leader of the people of Bristol. This is clearly evident after revealing the seaport's deep economic commitment to DeWolf and his successful career. It is thought provoking to note that the United States consistently refused to acknowledge the failure of so many attempts at slave trading laws written in its statute books during DeWolf's lifetime. The denial to put into place an active enforcement mechanism domestically or internationally prior to the Civil War is contemptible and seemingly motivated by greed.[356]

Correcting the mythology previously written about DeWolf and the state of Rhode Island has shown how he kidnapped, murdered and continually circumvented laws while successfully avoiding arrest both domestically and internationally. Ultimately, he had the innate ability to circumvent any law that was put into place and to successfully continue his involvement in the transatlantic slave trade from 1784 until the end of his life. Furthermore, DeWolf has not been held accountable historically for the delivery of thousands of Africans into the life of slavery. Despite all of these facts, James DeWolf has not been given a prominent place in United States history.

The most important testament of James DeWolf's current place in our country's narrative, and in the local seaport village of Bristol, can be seen by walking through his private cemetery. The land that DeWolf designated for his family graveyard, where his father, mother and multiple relatives are buried, was once on the edge of his acreage, the Mount. The cemetery is surrounded by a hand-built wall of stone—much like the ones built by slaves on his Cuban plantations. As you enter through a doublewide handcrafted wrought-iron gate leading onto a recently mowed path of grass and straight ahead of you, off in the distance you can see a hill. This is where the grand tomb of DeWolf and his wife stands, farthest from the street. It is unadorned with no markings to indicate its location; it is completely unassuming with the exception of an unmarked iron door that is nearly hidden by dirt and leaves. The tomb remains today, unattended, overgrown and nearly forgotten, much like this man's place in history.

Appendix

SLAVE TRADE LAWS

1784—(STATE) Rhode Island Gradual Emancipation Act was proposed and eventually passed. It stated that all blacks born after March 1, 1784, were to be free; slaves between the ages of fifteen to twenty-five would become indentured servants and freed after seven years; and slaves twenty-five and older would remain slaves for life.[357]

1787—(STATE) Rhode Island General Assembly, passed in November, imposed a fine on any shipowner who was caught importing slaves into Rhode Island.[358]

1790—(FEDERAL) Act of Congress: "That if any person or persons whatsoever shall, upon the high seas, commit the crime of piracy, as defined by the law of nations, and such offender or offenders shall be brought into, or found in the United States, every such offender or offenders shall, upon conviction thereof, be punished with death."[359]

1794—(FEDERAL) Federal Slave Trade Act was a revision to an act of Congress originally written in 1790.[360] The law stated that it was (still) illegal for any citizen of the United States to have any involvement in the slave trade to or from any foreign place or country and that fitting out of slaving ships in the United States for a foreign country was outlawed. If caught in violation of this law, the penalties included immediate ship forfeiture, a fine of $1,000 for each person involved and a fine of $200 for each slave who was transported. Building a slave vessel or promoting a slave venture resulted in a fine of $20,000.[361]

1800—(FEDERAL) Revision to Federal Slave Trade Act of 1794 added an amendment to the law of 1794. In addition to prohibiting the transport of slaves from the United States to any foreign country, outfitting a ship for the purposes of importing slaves or being employed in the slave trade, there was now a two-year prison term and an additional $100 fine per crew member for American citizens serving voluntarily on slavers added to the law.[362] Sections 27 and 28 of the law state the fine of $1,000 and forfeiture of all freight on board and that the freight's value would be determined, then tripled and fined as such. Section 50 addressed landing a vessel at night while evading entry in the customhouse. The fines included $200 per crew member, additional forfeiture of goods and forfeiture of the vessel.[363] A fine of $200 per crew member would have been equivalent to approximately $3,000 each in the early twenty-first century.[364]

1803—(FEDERAL) Revision to Federal Slave Trade Act of 1794 increased the penalties for United States citizens if caught slaving. It stated, "A penalty of one thousand dollars for each person brought to the United States on a ship with the intention of selling them as a slave." This law additionally placed responsibility on the captain of any vessel transporting slaves. It also charged customs and revenue officials in the government with enforcing this law, which was an indirect warning to those who might be in the best position for aiding illegal slave traders, such as Collector Collins of Bristol.[365]

1803—(STATE) South Carolina reopened its ports to the slave trade. It was illegal to trade slaves in South Carolina from 1787 to 1792, but the Act of 1792 was formally repealed and put into place in 1803. Rhode Island took advantage of this and funneled 80 percent of the slaves sold throughout the nation through the port of Charleston.[366]

1808—(FEDERAL) The International Trade of slavery was legally banned in the United States. This law stated that the importation of slaves into the United States, or its territories, was forbidden. It is another revision to the original law written in 1794, which was also revised in 1800 and 1803. The penalties recorded an increase in fines ranging from $5,000 to $25,000, forfeiture of the ship and, for the first time, imprisonment of five to ten years for all of the crew. This law also stated that if anyone was caught "outfitting, loading, or preparing any ship or vessel in any port or jurisdiction of the United States or caused any ship or vessel to sail from any port or place within the same, for the purpose of procuring any person to be transported or sold into slavery," the same penalties would be applied. Section 4 of this law stated that it was also illegal to "take on board, receive or transport from any of the coasts or kingdoms of Africa, or from any other foreign kingdom, place, or country," or any slave to be sold within the jurisdiction of the United States.[367]

1818—(FEDERAL) Revision to 1808, passed on April 20, 1818, reiterated the importance of the 1808 law. It stated that it was prohibited to bring slaves into any port or place within the jurisdiction of the United States. It was to prevent the introduction of slaves into the United States from other countries.[368]

1819—(FEDERAL) Act of Neutrality was ratified. The United States Congress passed legislation that stiffened provisions against American participation in the slave trade. It was considered an act of piracy for any American to outfit or serve a vessel for an insurgent colony *or* to join Colombian rebels *or* to transport slaves. If caught participating in any of these infractions, it was considered piracy and punishable by death *or* expulsion from the United States.[369]

1820—(FEDERAL) Revision to 1808. As a result of a slave vessel landing in the United States because of famishing conditions among the people on board, this revision was ratified. In the execution of laws relating to the importation of slaves, restitution of property condemned by the United States ought never to be made except in cases that are purged of every intentional violation of the law by proof of the most clear and most explicit and unequivocal nature.[370]

NOTES

PREFACE

1. Jacobs, *Incidents in the Life of a Slave Girl*, 34.

INTRODUCTION

2. Madison, *The Papers of James Madison, Vol. II*, April 2, 1787.
3. Coughtry, *Notorious Triangle*, 177.
4. Robinson, *Slavery in the Structure of American Politics*.
5. Greene, *Negro in Colonial New England*, 30.
6. Conley, *Liberty and Justice*, 167.
7. Mannix, *History of the Atlantic Slave Trade*, 164.
8. Ibid., 165.
9. Coughtry, *Notorious Triangle*, 25.
10. The DeWolf family name made several spelling transitions ending with the present spelling. Variations of the name can be found throughout multiple sources with references on the transitions of spelling. The family name can be seen spelled as D'Wolf, D'Wolfe, DeWoolfe, DeWolfe and today's spelling, DeWolf. For the purpose of this book, the present-day spelling is used.
11. Howe, *Mount Hope*, 70.
12. Farrow et al, *Complicity*, 103.
13. Mary Millard, e-mail message to author, August 9, 2013.
14. Ibid. The communion service was locked away in 1965 to keep it from being stolen during the civil rights era. It was a reaction by the church to the Watts Riots, nearly three thousand miles away in Los Angeles.

15. Pope-Hennessy, *Sins of our Fathers*, 239.

16. Rawley and Behrendt, *Transatlantic Slave Trade*, 328.

17. Thomas, *Slave Trade*, 535.

18. "James DeWolf," January 6, 2009, http://bioguide.congress.gov.

19. Appendix, Law of 1808.

20. Mary Millard, e-mail message; St. Michael's, *Vital Records of Rhode Island.*

CHAPTER 1

21. Conley, *Liberty and Justice*, 213.

22. Rediker, *Slave Ship*,101.

23. James DeWolf Deposition, June 15, 1791, Newport Historical Society (NHS).

24. Ibid.

25. Ibid.

26. Ibid.

27. *Polly* ship log, DeWolf Collection, Bristol Historical and Preservation Society (BHPS).

28. Howe, *Mount Hope*, 105.

29. Ellery, Letter Book #4, NHS.

30. DeWolf Deposition, June 15, 1791, NHS.

31. Ibid.

32. Appendix , Law of 1787.

33. Ibid., Law of 1790.

34. Conley, *Rhode Island's Founders*, 138.

35. Farrow et al, *Complicity*, 102.

36. *Providence Gazette and Country Journal*, James DeWolf Commentary, June 25, 1791. The article confirmed that the warrant had, by the date of publication, been issued.

37. *Newport Herald*, February 3, 1791, 4.

38. Conley, *Liberty and Justice*, 213; Howe, *Mt. Hope*, 106.

39. Eltis, "Trans-Atlantic Slave Trade," *Nancy*, #36773; Peck and Bradford family trees.

40. James DeWolf, Insurance File, October 21, 1801, BHPS.

41. Rawley, *Transatlantic Slave Trade*, 269.

42. Paiewonsky, *Eyewitness Accounts*, 48.

CHAPTER 2

43. Shepherd and Beckles, *Caribbean Slavery*, 585.

44. Jameson, "St. Eustatius," 683.

45. Ayisi, *St. Eustatius*, 113.
46. Parry et al, *Short History of the West Indies*, 183–84.
47. Shepherd and Beckles, *Caribbean Slavery*, 584–85.
48. Rediker, *Slave Ship*, 44.
49. Eltis et al, "Slave Prices," 676.
50. Schiltkamp and DeSmidt, *St. Maarten, St. Eustatius, Saba*, 387.
51. Ron Wetteroth, e-mail message to author, July 16, 2009.
52. Goslinga, *Short History*, 82.
53. Ibid., 83.
54. Ayisi, *St. Eustatius*, 40; Jameson, "St. Eustatius," 683.
55. Ayisi, *St. Eustatius*, 8–9, 690.
56. Ibid., 13.
57. Jameson, "St. Eustatius," 684.
58. Ayisi, *St. Eustatius*, 38.
59. Goslinga, *Short History*, 86.
60. Ayisi, *St. Eustatius*, 160.
61. Eltis, TASTD.
62. James DeWolf to John DeWolf, receipt dated July 1, 1795, BHPS. In the amount of $520.04, with interest.
63. John DeWolf, receipts file between John and James DeWolf, varying dates, BHPS.
64. Nancy Kougeas, e-mail message to author, September 7, 2009; DeWolf receipts file, varying dates, BHPS.
65. Paiewonsky, *Eyewitness Accounts*, 61.
66. James DeWolf Deposition, October 2, 1794, NHS.
67. Rediker, *Slave Ship*, 414.
68. *Judge Jay* through *Snow Dove*, ships folder, BHPS; James DeWolf, Letter to Levi DeWolf, August 8, 1792, BHPS.
69. James DeWolf, Letter to Levi DeWolf, August 8, 1792, DeWolf Family Papers, Mss 382, Reel 9, Rhode Island Historical Society (RIHS).
70. Wetteroth, *St. Eustatius*. Wetteroth is the creator of the St. Eustatius database of names that lists the first known residents on the island beginning with a party of about thirty to forty people until present day. The database includes more than fifteen thousand names, researched through church and local records. This particular West Indian island was unoccupied in 1636, when the Dutch first arrived. The records of the First Dutch West India Company disappeared after its bankruptcy in the 1670s. The records start to pick up in the 1680s with the Second Dutch Company. Wetteroth noted that there were many crew members from ships that came and went from Statia as a result of its very active port. Many sailors were referred to as transients (a common term used in Statia) because they did not appear in any other known Statia documents. Surprisingly, Wetteroth found that there were a

number of marriage records for sailors marrying Statia women; however, according to Wetteroth, Stockman and Claning did not fall into this category, which is why they were referred to as transients.

71. Rediker, *Slave Ship*, 413.
72. DeWolf Deposition, June 15, 1791, DeWolf Family Papers, Mss 382, Reel 9, RIHS.
73. James DeWolf Deposition, October 2, 1794, NHS.
74. DeWolf Deposition, June 15, 1791, DeWolf Family Papers, Mss 382, Reel 9, RIHS.
75. James DeWolf Deposition, October 2, 1794, NHS.
76. DeWolf Deposition, June 15, 1791, DeWolf Family Papers, Mss 382, Reel 9, RIHS.
77. Paiewonsky, *Eyewitness Accounts*, 61.
78. James DeWolf correspondence, August 8, 1794, BHPS.
79. Paiewonsky, *Eyewitness Accounts*, 61.
80. Ibid., 75.
81. Ibid., 69 and 71.
82. Goslinga, *Short History*, 86.
83. Eltis, TASTD, *Sally*, #36616.
84. Rediker, *Slave Ship*, 346.
85. Ibid., 346; Table 1.
86. Conley, *Rhode Island's Founders*, 141
87. United States Federal Census Records, 1790.
88. Rediker, *Slave Ship*, 346.

Chapter 3

89. Fowler, *William Ellery*, 12, 16.
90. Appendix, Law of 1784.
91. Conley, *Liberty and Justice*, 179.
92. Ibid., 201.
93. Rawley, *Transatlantic Slave Trade*, 307.
94. Thomas, *Slave Trade*, 502.
95. Ibid., 482; Appendix, Law of 1784.
96. Appendix, Law of 1787.
97. Bartlett, *From Slave to Citizen*, 333.
98. Hamm, "American Slave Trade," 84.
99. Coleman, "Entrepreneurial Spirit," 321; Rawley, *Transatlantic Slave Trade*, 269.
100. Robinson, *Slavery*, 57.
101. Eltis, TASTD.

102. Anstey, *Atlantic Slave Trade*, 28.

103. Thorton, *Africa and Africans*, 192.

104. Haskins and Benson, *Bound for America*, 31.

105. Klein, *Atlantic Slave Trade*, 132.

106. Coughtry, *Notorious Triangle*, 145; DeWolf Ship Files, BHPS.

107. Anstey, *Atlantic Slave*, 28.

108. Paiewonsky, *Eyewitness Accounts*, 45.

109. Hamm, *American Slave*, 205.

110. Ibid., 250.

111. Farrow, *Complicity*, 111.

112. Claire Benson private collection, Bristol, Rhode Island.

113. John DeWolf, Letter to Levi DeWolf, January 21, 1799, and Levi DeWolf to James DeWolf, February 11, 1806, DeWolf Family Papers, Mss 382, Reel 9, RIHS.

114. Reynolds, *Stand the Storm*, 73.

115. Thomas, *Slave Trade*, 535.

116. Coughtry, *Notorious Triangle*, 212.

117. DeWolf Business Files, Bank of Bristol, BHPS.

118. Tracy Nelson, "Wharf Research" (Roger Williams University, 1999); Bank of Bristol, DeWolf Collection, Mss382, Reel 9, RIHS.

119. Historic and Architectural Resources of Bristol, Rhode Island, 15.

120. Hamm, *American Slave*, 103; Derks and Smith, *Value of a Dollar*, 253; Nelson, "Wharf Research."

121. Bordo and Schwartz, "Performance and Stability."

122. Hesselberg, "Shipwreck Takes Town." Although it is common knowledge in the historical world that stones were used as ballast, it was most recently confirmed through this article regarding a vessel from 1812.

123. A Dictionary of Units of Measure.

124. DeWolf Ships Files, BHPS.

125. Mainememory.net; Swensongranite.com, September 9, 2012; Fall River Historical Society, lizziborden.org, November 24, 2012.

126. Brayley, *History of the Granite Industry*, 137–38.

127. Paiewonsky, *Eyewitness Accounts*, 73.

128. Hedges, *Browns of Providence Plantations*, 103.

129. James DeWolf, Bristol Insurance Company, BHPS.

130. Davis, "Living off the Trade," 3.

131. Thomas, *Slave Ship*, 312.

132. Coughtry, *Notorious Triangle*, 95.

133. James DeWolf, Insurance file, October 21,1801, BHPS.

134. Ibid.

135. Hamm, *American Slave*, 106.

136. Hedges, *Browns of Providence*, 103.

CHAPTER 4

137. Coughtry, *Notorious Triangle*, 264.

138. Howe, *Mount Hope*, 102.

139. Mary Millard, e-mail message to author, September 6, 2009. "Some of the family went to the Congregational Church but most of them went to the Episcopal Church." She also stated: "Levi and his wife attended the Congregational Church," according to church records, which disputes the Quaker theory.

140. Mary Millard, e-mail message. As a direct descendant of Levi DeWolf, Mrs. Millard has inherited his Bible, book collection and private papers; Congregational Church, *Vital Record of Rhode Island*.

141. James DeWolf Business Records, BHPS.

142. James DeWolf, Letter to Levi DeWolf, August 8, 1792, DeWolf Family Papers, Mss 382, Reel 9, RIHS.

143. Howe, *Mount Hope*, 101, 102, 112, 130, 136, 202, 221, 273, 277, 283. A privately held collection of Levi's letters were shared with the author for the first time in 2010, which helped to confirm this information, along with archived documents from BHPS, RIHS and Baker Library, Harvard.

144. James DeWolf, Letter to Levi DeWolf, October 26, 1794, DeWolf Family Papers, Mss 382, Reel 9, RIHS.

145. Ibid., October (no day noted), 1794.

146. Eltis, TASTD.

147. James DeWolf ships logs, BHPS.

148. James DeWolf, Letter to Levi DeWolf, December 16, 1791, DeWolf Family Papers, Mss 382, Reel 9, RIHS.

149. Mary Millard, private collection, Bristol, Rhode Island.

150. James DeWolf, Letter to Levi DeWolf, August 31, 1793, DeWolf Family Papers, Mss 382, Reel 9, RIHS.

151. Mary Millard, private collection. Additional letters written by Levi while he was delivering cargo to Havana are dated February 1797 and December 1801.

152. James DeWolf, Letter to Levi DeWolf, January 20, 1800, DeWolf Family Papers, Mss 382, Reel 9, RIHS.

153. Nancy Kougeus, "DeWolf Cuban Plantations," October 13, 2010.

154. James DeWolf, Letter to Levi DeWolf, January 20, 1800, DeWolf Family Papers, Mss 382, Reel 9, RIHS.

155. Ibid.

156. Mary Millard, private collection, letter dated December 14, 1801.

157. Levi DeWolf, Letter to Lydia DeWolf, February 11, 1806, DeWolf Family Papers, Mss 382, Reel 9, RIHS.

158. James DeWolf Business Records, BHPS.

159. Eltis, TASTD, voyage #36905.

CHAPTER 5

160. Appendix.

161. Fowler, *William Ellery*, 1.

162. Pelton, *Men of Destiny*, 91. It was reported that Ellery recognized the personal risk that all of the signers were taking and chose to stand very close to the signing table in order to witness the expression each man had on his face at the time he displayed his signature.

163. Fowler, *William Ellery*, 7.

164. Ibid., 83, 144, 146, 150. Included in the Rufus King papers, found at the New York Historical Society, letters can be found that reference James DeWolf and his slaving activities. Interestingly, King also held a copy of the deposition in his personal collection of papers that was written in Newport and resulted in a warrant for DeWolf's arrest for the charge of murder.

165. Fowler, *William Ellery*, 152.

166. Ibid., 170–71.

167. Conley, *Rhode Island's Founders*, 139.

168. Fowler, *William Ellery*, 172.

169. Farrow, *Complicity*, 111.

170. Government Port Surveyor, www.seaload.net, June 5, 2009.

171. William Ellery, Letter to Samuel Bosworth, June 16, 1794, U.S. Custom House, Britol-Warren, Item 2, Box 1, RIHS.

172. Simeon Potter, Letter to James DeWolf, May 2, 1794, DeWolf Family Papers, Mss 382, Reel 9, RIHS.

173. Coughtry, *Notorious Triangle*, 177.

174. Coleman, "Entrepreneurial Spirit," 336. John Brown was one of the few charged with violating the 1794 act.

175. Eltis, *Economic Growth*, 107; Mount Hope; Kougeus, "DeWolf Cuban Plantations," BHPS.

176. James DeWolf, ships log. Each entry varies slightly according to date and the person who placed the slave request. There is a fee listed for each slave and then additional charges on the bottom line of the ledger that are incorporated into the total cost. Some requests can be found in the receipts file on small slips of paper; McMillan, *Final Victims*, 73.

177. *Juno*, undated, 1796, DeWolf Papers, BHPS.

178. Ibid.

179. Coughtry, *Notorious Triangle*, 146.

180. Hamm, *American Slave*, 88.

181. Bristol, Rhode Island, www.onlinebristol.com, June 5, 2009.

182. Coughtry, *Notorious Triangle*, 225.

183. Farrow, *Complicity*, 110.

184. Coughtry, *Notorious Triangle*, 225.

185. McMillan, *Final Victims*, 38.

186. Thomas, *Slave Trade*, 579.
187. Department of Revenue, www.dor.ri.gov, June 5, 2009. Customhouses charged revenue that was garnered for both local and federal funding. Districts were determined by population and divided up accordingly.

CHAPTER 6

188. Howe, *Mount Hope*, 108.
189. David L. Barnes, Letter to William Ellery, May 11, 1799, Channing-Ellery Papers, Mss 341, Folder 33, Vol. 6, RIHS.
190. Eltis, TASTD, vessel #36690.
191. Coughtry, *Notorious Triangle*, 272.
192. Farrow, *Complicity*, 111.
193. Coughtry, *Notorious Triangle*, 272.
194. Rappleye, *Sons of Providence*, 317.
195. William Ellery, Letter to Samuel Bosworth, June 16, 1794, U.S. Custom House, Bristol-Warren, Box 1, Item 2, RIHS.
196. Samuel Bosworth, www.ancestry.com; Table 1.
197. Rappleye, *Sons of Providence*, 317.
198. Ibid., 318.
199. Coughtry, *Notorious Triangle*, 217.
200. Howe, *Mount Hope*, 108.
201. Coughtry, *Notorious Triangle*, 218.
202. Oliver Wolcott, United States Treasury Department, Letter to William Ellery, August 5, 1799, U.S. Custom House, Bristol-Warren, Box 1, Item 3, RIHS.
203. William Ellery, Letter to David Barnes, July 8, 1799, U.S. Custom House, Bristol-Warren, Box 1, Item 2, RIHS.
204. Thomas, *Slave Trade*, 603.
205. Eltis, TASTD #36690.
206. Eltis, *Economic Growth*, 107.
207. William Ellery, Letter to David Barnes, October 15, 1799, Channing-Ellery Papers, Mss 341, Folder 35, Vol. 6, RIHS.
208. David Barnes, Letter to William Ellery, November 1799, Channing-Ellery Papers, Mss 341, Folder 37, Vol. 6, RIHS.
209. Appendix, Law of 1800; Hamm, *American Slave*, 90.
210. Jefferson, "Papers," 671.
211. Coleman, "Entrepreneurial Spirit," 322.
212. John Brown, Letter to "Friend," 1800, John Brown Papers, 1736–1803, Mss 312, Box 1, Folder 25, RIHS.
213. Rappleye, *Sons of Providence*, 334.

CHAPTER 7

214. Charles Collins, Letter to John DeWolf, October 22, 1803, DeWolf Family Papers, Mss 382, Reel 9, RIHS.

215. Risjord, *Early American Party Systems*, 153.

216. Ibid., 154.

217. Howe, *Mount Hope*, 108.

218. Coleman, "Entrepreneurial Spirit," 334.

219. Eltis, *Trans-Atlantic*, voyage #36757.

220. Cunningham, *Jeffersonian Republicans*, 27.

221. Banning, *Jeffersonian Persuasion*, 276.

222. Risjord, *Early American*, 157.

223. Jefferson, *Jefferson Letters*, vol. 33, 663.

224. Charles Collins, Letter to John DeWolf, October 22, 1803, DeWolf Family Papers, Mss 382, Reel 9, RIHS.

225. Eltis, TASTD, #36780. The DeWolf vessel the *Amastad* is not to be confused with the famous *La Amistad* of nearly forty years later and so powerfully portrayed through literature and a Hollywood screenplay.

226. Charles Collins, Letter to John DeWolf, October 22, 1803, DeWolf Family Papers, Mss 382, Reel 9, RIHS.

227. Ibid.

228. Ibid.

229. Ibid.

230. Ibid.

231. Ibid.

232. Ibid.

233. Coughtry, *Notorious Triangle*, 228.

234. Freeling, "Founding Fathers and Slavery," 84; Coleman, "Entrepreneurial Spirit," 335.

235. Coleman, "Entrepreneurial Spirit," 334.

236. Thomas, *Slave Trade*, 545; Appendix, Law of 1800; Eltis, TASTD, #36782.

237. D'Wolfe, *Bristol, Rhode Island*, 81.

238. U.S. Custom House, Bristol-Warren, Mss 28, Sub-group 2, Box 3, RIHS.

239. Coughtry, *Notorious Triangle*, 228.

240. Ibid., 226.

241. Thomas, *Slave Trade*, 603.

242. Ibid., 545.

243. Hamm, *American Slave*, 102.

244. U.S. Custom House, Bristol-Warren, Mss 28, Sub-group 2, Box 4, RIHS.

245. James DeWolf Business Records, Baker Library Historical Collections, Mss 766, Box 1, Harvard Business School.

CHAPTER 8

246. Appendix, Law of 1808. South Carolina had originally passed an antislaving law on a trial basis in 1787 but repealed it in 1803.

247. Eltis, TASTD, #36780.

248. Appendix, Law of 1800.

249. Coughtry, *Notorious Triangle*, 228.

250. *Amastad*, U.S. Custom House, Bristol-Warren, Mss 28, Sub-group 2, Box 3, RIHS.

251. *Minerva*, U.S. Custom House, Bristol-Warren, Mss 28, Sub-group 2, Box 3, RIHS.

252. "African Slave Trade," National Archives and Records Administration, www.morrow.resources@nara.gov.

253. Eltis, TASTD, #37251.

254. Donnan, "New England Slave Trade," 254.

255. Davis, "Teaching the Truth," 3. Federal laws apply to the nation as a whole; state laws affect just the particular state where they were ratified. However, a state law can be superior or subordinate to a federal law, giving state residents more rights and, ultimately, the power to overrule a federal law. This was the case in South Carolina when it repealed its original state law toward the slave trade. The federal government had difficulty influencing states' rights until the Emancipation Proclamation was written in 1863.

256. McMillin, *Final Victims*, 130.

257. Eltis,TASTD, #36890.

258. McMillin, *Final Victims*, 130.

259. Thomas, *Slave Ship*, 545.

260. Eltis.TASTD, #36881; Howe, *Mount Hope*, 129. Family historian George Howe stated in his book that James DeWolf left on his final voyage in 1807, returning just days before Christmas of the same year, when in fact he left in June 1806, returning to Bristol in the fall of 1807.

261. Coughtry, *Notorious Triangle*, 76.

262. Ibid., 69.

263. Eltis,TASTD,#36881.

264. Ibid.

265. James DeWolf, ships log, *Andromache*, page number illegible but most likely 212, BHPS.

266. Eltis, TASTD, #36881.

267. James DeWolf, ships log, *Andromache*, 214, BHPS.

268. Howe, *Mount Hope*, 128. Many historical accounts have the two DeWolf slave children's names spelled as they would appear phonetically. Family historian George Howe stated that the slaves were buried in the DeWolf family cemetery. However, Pauledore's stone has yet to be found.

269. James D'Wolf, United States federal census, 1810, www.AncestoryLibrary. com. In 1810, census records required only an approximation of age for all "Free White Males and Females" living in the household, with only one column for an accounting of slaves owned.

270. James D'Wolf, United States federal census, 1820, www. AncestoryLibrary.com.

271. Pauledore D'Wolf, United States federal census, 1830, www. AncestoryLibrary.com.

272. D'Wolfe, *Bristol, Rhode Island*, 107.

273. DeWolf Private Cemetery, Bristol, Rhode Island; Matthew C. Perry and Ray Payson, both DeWolf descendants, carefully and diligently cleaned, repaired and reset the stones of the two slave women in March 2013.

274. Pauledore D'Wolf, United States federal census, 1870, www. AncestoryLibrary.com.

275. Thompson, *Sketches of Old Bristol*, 103.

276. Howe, *Mount Hope*, 196.

277. *Three Sisters* ledger, October 12, 1807, DeWolf Papers, Mss 382, Reel 9, RIHS.

278. Ibid.

279. Scott and Smith, *Value of a Dollar*, 253.

CHAPTER 9

280. Thomas, *Slave Trade*, 552; Stafford, "Illegal Importations," 124.

281. Mannix, *Black Cargoes*, 190.

282. James DeWolf ship logs, BHPS.

283. St. Michael's Church, "Vital Records of Rhode Island," Bristol, Rhode Island.

284. James DeWolf Business Records, Baker Library Historical Collection, Mss 766, Box 1, Harvard Business School.

285. U.S. Custom House, Bristol-Warren, Mss 28, Sub-group 2, Box 4, RIHS.

286. James DeWolf ships logs, BHPS.

287. Coughtry, *Notorious Triangle*, 233.

288. Kiple, "Case Against," 346.

289. Channing-Ellery Papers, Mss 341, Folders 107, 109, and 191, Vol. 6, RIHS.

290. Eltis, TASTD, #36928. Only ninety-five slaves survived this journey.

291. Coleman, "Entrepreneurial Spirit," 335.

292. Mannix, *Black Cargoes*, 190.

293. Charles Clarke Letter to "Mamma", January 17, 1808, BHPS.

294. Ibid.

295. United States Treasury Department correspondence, August 10, 1808, U.S. Custom House, Bristol-Warren, Box 4, Item 10-11, RIHS.

296. Surveyor of Warren correspondence, October 23, 1808, U.S. Custom House, Bristol-Warren, Box 4, Item 9, RIHS.

297. William Ellery correspondence, November 10, 1808, U.S. Custom House, Bristol-Warren, Box 4, Item 10-11, RIHS. Outfitting ships for the slave trade was all that was needed to impound a vessel and arrest the crew. It was not necessary to actually see the slaves.

298. William Ellery correspondence, December 24, 1808, U.S. Custom House, Bristol-Warren, Box 4, Item 13-15, RIHS.

299. William Ellery, Letter Book, January 29, 1810–June 30, 1818, NHS.

300. Conley, *Liberty and Justice*, 167.

301. Gallatin, *Bristol County Register*.

302. Rappleye, *Sons of Providence*, 338.

303. Stafford, "Illegal Importations," 125.

304. Thomas, *Slave Trade*, 569.

305. Stafford, "Illegal Importations," 133.

306. Coleman, "The Entrepreneurial Spirit," 334.

307. Madison, "Captures of American Vessels," 562.

308. D'Wolfe, *Bristol, Rhode Island*, 81.

309. John DeWolf Correspondence file, BHPS. Once again, the correspondence confirmed continued illegal involvement in the slave trade by the DeWolfs.

310. William Ellery correspondence, December (no day), 1815; Letter Book, January 29, 1810–June 30, 1818, NHS.

311. Ibid.

312. Ibid.

313. Ibid.; Howe.*Mount Hope*, 212.

314. William Ellery correspondence, December (no day), 1815; Letter Book, January 29, 1810–June 30, 1818, NHS.

315. Ibid.

316. James DeWolf Business Records, Baker Library Historical Collections, Mss. 766, Box 1, Harvard Business School.

317. James DeWolf, Letter to John DeWolf, January 6, 1816, Letter Book; January 29, 1810–June 30, 1818, NHS.

318. William Ellery, Letter to Charles Collins, February 1, 1816; Letter Book; January 29, 1810–June 30, 1818, NHS.

319. Ibid.

320. Coleman, "Entrepreneurial Spirit," 334. It would not be surprising if there were still a multitude of forgotten archives collecting dust in the attics or cellars of many homes in Bristol.

321. Howe, *Mount Hope*, 205.

CHAPTER 10

322. James DeWolf Business Records, Baker Library Historical Collections, Mss. 766, Box 1, Harvard Business School.

323. Spanish Treaty of 1817, www.nationalarchives.gov.

324. James DeWolf Business Records, Baker Library Historical Collections, Mss. 766, Box 1, Harvard Business School.

325. Ibid.

326. Ibid.

327. Ibid.

328. James Monroe, April 20, 1818, Gilder Lehrman Collection, New York.

329. Committee on Foreign Relations, May 19, 1824, Gilder Lehrman Collection, New York.

330. Thomas, *Slave Trade*, 603.

331. James DeWolf correspondence, 1818, BHPS.

332. Charles Collins, Letter to James DeWolf, February (no date), 1819, DeWolf Family Papers, Mss 382, Reel 9, RIHS. Rhode Islanders referred to their Cuban plantations as "estates."

333. Ibid.

334. Goodrich, *Lives of the Signers*, 186.

335. Conley, *Rhode Island Founders*, 186.

336. Andreas. *Smuggler Nation*, 139.

337. Thomas, *Slave Trade*, 618.

338. James DeWolf, Letter to Frances Diman, October 15, 1821, DeWolf Family Papers, Mss 382, Reel 9, RIHS.

339. Charles Collins, Letter to James DeWolf, October 19, 1821, DeWolf Family Papers, Mss 382, Reel 9, RIHS.

340. James DeWolf Business Records, Baker Library Historical Collections, Mss. 766, Box 1, Harvard Business School.

341. Howe, *Mount Hope*, 192.

342. "James DeWolf," www.bioguide.congress.gov, January 6, 2009.

343. Higman, *Slave Populations*, 275.

344. James DeWolf, Letter to Captain Bradford, September (no date), 1826, DeWolf Family Papers, Mss 382, Reel 10, RIHS. Once DeWolf became involved with owning his own plantations in Cuba, the term "slave" transitioned to "Negro," even though they were still slaves.

345. James DeWolf, Letter to Captain Bradford, September (no date), 1826, DeWolf Family Papers, Mss 382, Reel 10, RIHS.

346. Mark Anthony DeWolf, Letter to Captain Bradford, October (no date), 1826, DeWolf Family Papers, Mss 382, Reel 10, RIHS.

347. Ibid.

348. Captain Bradford, Letter to James DeWolf, April 4, 1829, DeWolf Family Papers, Mss 382, Reel 10, RIHS.

349. DeWolf correspondence, 1833, BHPS.

EPILOGUE

350. Griswold, *Discourse Delivered in Bristol*, 39.

351. Ibid., 4.

352. Ibid., 10.

353. Ibid., 11–12.

354. Ibid., 12.

355. Ibid.

356. Stafford, "Illegal Importations," 125.

APPENDIX

357. Conley, *Liberty and Justice*, 179.

358. Donnan, *Documents Illustrative*, vol. III, 343; Thomas, *Slave Trade*, 502.

359. Eltis et al., "Slave Prices," 676; McCarthur, *Seaman's Contract*.

360. McCarthur, *Seaman's Contract*, 190.

361. Hamm, *American Slave*, 88.

362. Coughtry, *Notorious Triangle*, 212.

363. Channing-Ellery Papers, Mss341, Folder 77, Vol. 6, RIHS.

364. Scott and Smith, *Value of a Dollar*, 253.

365. "The African Slave Trade," National Archives and Records Administration, www.morrow.resources@nara.gov, June 5, 2009, 2.

366. Farrow, *Complicity*, 111.

367. Grossman, *Spirit of American Law*, 62.

368. Department of Justice, Act of April 20, 1818, 3 Stat. 450, www.justice.gov.

369. "The African Slave Trade," National Archives and Records Administration, www.morrow.resources@nara.gov, June 5, 2009, 2.

370. Department of Justice, Act of May 15, 1820, 3 Stat. 600, www.justice.gov.

BIBLIOGRAPHY

PRIMARY SOURCES

Archives: Letters, Journal Entries, and Depositions

"The African Slave Trade." National Archives and Records Administration. Southeast Region, Atlanta, Georgia, 1985.

American State Papers 03, Foreign Relations, vol. 3, 12th Congress, 1st Session, Publication No. 246.

"Bosworth, Bradford, Ellery, and Peck" Family Trees. www. AncestoryLibrary.com.

Brown, John. John Brown Papers, 1736–1803. Mss 312, Box 1, Folder 25, Rhode Island Historical Society.

Channing-Ellery Papers,1760–1819. Mss 341, Box 6, Folders 7, 23, 25, 33, 35, 37, 39, 77, 107, 109, 191. Rhode Island Historical Society.

DeWolf Collection. Bristol Historical and Preservation Society, Rhode Island.

DeWolf Family Collection. Privately held, Mary Millard. Bristol, Rhode Island.

DeWolf Family Papers, 1751–1864. Mss 382. Papers of the American Slave Trade, Series A, Part 2, Reels 9 and 10, Rhode Island Historical Society.

Eltis, David. "A Brief Overview of the Trans-Atlantic Slave Trade." Voyages: The Trans-Atlantic Slave Trade Database. http://www.slavevoyages.org.

First Congregational Church, Bristol, Rhode Island. *Vital Record of Rhode Island, 1636–1850.* Births, Marriages and Deaths. Narragansett, RI: Narragansett Historical Publishing Company, 1906.

Jacobs, Harriet. *Incidents in the Life of a Slave Girl Written by Herself.* Boston: published for the author, 1861.

James DeWolf Business Records. Baker Library Historical Collections. Mss 766, Box 1-2. Harvard Business School.

James D'Wolf Deposition. Box 43, Folder 24. Newport Historical Society, Rhode Island.

"James D'Wolf," 1790–1840. United States Federal Census. www.AncestoryLibrary.com.

Joseph Goodwin Diary, 1820–1827. MS569, series II, V, VIII. New York Historical Society, New York.

Madison, James. "Captures of American Wessels by the Belligerents. Communicated to Congress, April 23, 1812."

———. "The Papers of James Madison, Vol. II." Washington, D.C.: Langtree and O'Sullivan, 1840.

Manzano, Juan Francisco. *Autobiography of a Slave/Autobiografía de un Esclavo.* Detroit, MI: Wayne State University Press, 1996.

McCarther, Walter, ed. *The Seaman's Contract, 1790–1918.* Washington, D.C.: Congress of the United States, n.d.

"Nathaniel Smith." *Memorials of Connecticut Judges and Attorneys as Printed in the Connecticut Reports.* Vol. 15, appendix, 32–33.

Oberg, Barbara B., ed. *The Papers of Thomas Jefferson.* Vol. 35. Princeton, NJ: Princeton University Press, 2008.

"Pauledore D'Wolf," 1800–1870. United States Federal Census. www.AncestoryLibrary.com.

Rufus King Papers. MS 1660. New York Historical Society, New York.

St. Michael's Episcopal Church, Bristol, Rhode Island. *Vital Record of Rhode Island, 1636–1850.* Births, Marriages and Deaths, Narragansett, RI: Narragansett Historical Publishing Company, 1906.

U.S. Customhouse Records, Bristol-Warren. Mss 28, Sub Group 2, Box 1, 2, 4, 5. Rhode Island Historical Society.

"Will for James D'Wolf of Bristol, Rhode Island." Will Book #4, 252-274. Town Hall, Bristol, Rhode Island.

"William Bradford, William Ellery, Thomas Jefferson, James Monroe, and the Committee on Foreign Relations." Gilder Lehrman Institute of American History, New York. www.gilderlehrman.org.

William Ellery Letter Book # 4, January 29, 1810–June 30, 1818. Newport Historical Society, Rhode Island.

Books

D'Wolf, John. *A Voyage to the North Pacific.* Cambridge, MA: Welch, Bigelow and Company, 1861.

Griswold, Alexander V. *A Discourse Delivered in Bristol, Rhode Island, February 11, 1838, Occasioned by the Deceased of the Hon. James D'Wolf and Mrs. Ann B. D'Wolf, His Wife.* Bristol, RI: W.H.S. Bayley, 1838.

Perry, Reverend Calbraith B. *Charles D'Wolf of Guadeloupe, His Ancestors and Descendants: Being a Complete Genealogy of the "Rhode Island D'Wolfs," The Descendants of Simon DeWolf, with Their Common Descent from Balthasar DeWolf, of Lyme Connecticut, 1668.* New York: Press of T.A. Wright, 1902.

SECONDARY SOURCES
Unpublished Research

Benson, Claire. "Bristol Cuba Connection Project." 2010–ongoing. Bristol Historical and Preservation Society.

Hamm, Tommy Todd. "The American Slave Trade with Africa, 1620–1807." PhD diss. Indiana University, 1975.

Kougeus, Nancy. "DeWolf Cuban Plantations." October 13, 2010. Private.

Nelson, Tracey. "Wharf Research." Roger Williams University, Rhode Island, 1999.

Documentary Film

Browne, Katrina, director, producer, author. *Traces of the Trade: A Story from the Deep North.* Documentary film, 2009.

Articles

Aiken, Susan Hardy. "An Incident in the Life of a Slaveholder: The Search for Nancy Gindrat." *New England Quarterly* 78, no. 1 (March 2005): 77–100.

Bordo, Michael D., and Anna J. Schwartz. "The Performance and Stability of Banking Systems Under Self-Regulation: Theory and Evidence." *Cato Journal* 14, no. 3 (July 24, 2009). www.cato.org.

Coleman, Peter J. "The Entrepreneurial Spirit in Rhode Island History." *Business History Review* 37, no. 4 (Winter 1963): 319–44.

Davis, David Brion. "Looking at Slavery from Broader Perspectives." *American Historical Review* 105, no. 2 (April 2000): 452–66.

Donnan, Elizabeth. "The New England Slave Trade after the Revolution." *New England Quarterly* 3, no. 2 (April 1930): 251–78.

Eltis, David, Frank D. Lewis and David Richardson. "Slave Prices, the African Slave Trade, and Productivity in the Caribbean, 1674–1807." *Economic History Review* 58, no. 4 (November 2005): 673–700.

Freeling, William W. "The Founding Fathers and Slavery." *American Historical Review* 77, no. 1 (February 1972): 81–93.

Jameson, J. Franklin. "St. Eustatius in the American Revolution." *American Historical Association* 8, no. 4 (July 1903): 683–708.

Kiple, Kenneth F. "The Case Against a Nineteenth-Century Cuba-Florida Slave Trade." *Florida Historical Quarterly* 49, no. 4 (April 1971): 346–55.

Lin, Rachel Chernos. "The Rhode Island Slave-Traders: Butchers, Bakers and Candlestick-Makers." *Slavery and Abolition* 23, no. 3 (December 2002): 21–38.

Lofton, Williston H. "Abolition and Labor: Reaction of Northern Labor to the Anti-Slavery Appeal." *Journal of Negro History* 33, no. 3 (July 1948): 261–83.

Sheridan, Richard B. "The Crisis of Slave Subsistence in the British West Indies During and After the American Revolution." *William and Mary Quarterly* 33, no. 4 (October 1976): 615–41.

Stafford, Frances J. "Illegal Importations: Enforcement of the Slave Trade Laws along the Florida Coast, 1810–1828." *Florida Historical Society* 46, no. 2 (October 1967): 124–33.

Books

Amar, Akhil Reed. *American's Constitution: A Biography.* New York: Random House, 2005.

Andreas, Peter. *Smuggler Nation: How Illicit Trade Made America.* New York: Oxford University Press, 2013.

Anstey, Roger. *The Atlantic Slave Trade and British Abolition, 1760–1810.* New Jersey: Humanities Press, 1975.

Atherton, Herbert M., and J. Jackson Barlow. *1791–1991 The Bill of Rights and Beyond.* Washington, D.C.: Library of Congress, 1990.

Ayisi, Eric O. *St. Eustatius: The Treasure Island of the Caribbean.* Trenton, NJ: Africa World Press, Inc., 1992.

Banning, Lance. *The Jeffersonian Persuasion, Evolution of a Party Ideology.* London: Cornell University Press, 1978.

Barboza, Steven. *Door of No Return: The Legend of Gorée Island.* New York: Cobblehill Books, 1994.

Barcia, Manuel. *The Great African Slave Revolt of 1825, Cuba and the Fight for Freedom in Matanzas.* Baton Rouge: Louisiana State University Press, 2012.

Bartlett, Irving H. *From Slave to Citizen.* Rhode Island: Urban League of Rhode Island, 1954.

Bowen, Catherine Drinker. *Miracle at Philadelphia: The Story of the Constitutional Convention May to September 1787.* Boston: Little, Brown and Company, 1966.

Brayley, Arthur Wellington. *History of Granite in New England.* Vol. 1. Boston: National Association of Granite Industries of the United States, 1913.

Chomsky, Aviva, Barry Carr, et al., eds. *The Cuba Reader: History, Culture, Politics.* Durham, NC: Duke University Press, 2003.

BIBLIOGRAPHY

Christopher, Emma. *Slave Ship Sailors and Their Captive Cargoes, 1730–1807.* Cambridge, UK: Cambridge University Press, 2006.

Conley, Patrick T. *Liberty and Justice: A History of Law and Lawyers in Rhode Island, 1636–1998.* East Providence: Rhode Island Publications Society, 1998.

———. *Rhode Island's Founders: Settlement to Statehood.* Charleston, SC: The History Press, 2010.

Coughtry, Jay. *The Notorious Triangle, Rhode Island and the African Slave Trade, 1700–1807.* Philadelphia: Temple University Press, 1981.

Cunningham, Noble E. *The Jeffersonian Republicans, The Formation of Party Organization, 1789–1801.* Chapel Hill: University of North Carolina Press, 1957.

Derks, Scott, and Tony Smith. *The Value of the Dollar: Colonial Era to the Civil War, 1600–1865.* New York: Grey House Publishing, 2005.

DeWolfe, Mark Anthony. *Bristol, Rhode Island: A Town Biography.* Cambridge, MA: Harvard University Press, 1930.

DeWolf, Thomas Norman. *Inheriting the Trade.* Boston: Beacon Press, 2008.

Donnan, Elizabeth. *Documents Illustrative of the History of the Slave Trade to America.* Vol. III, *New England and the Middle Colonies.* Washington, D.C.: Carnegie Institution of Washington, 1932.

DuBois, W.E.B. *The Suppression of the African Slave-Trade to the United States, 1638–1870.* New York: Russell & Russell, 1898.

Elliott, J.H. *Empires of the Atlantic World: Britain and Spain in American, 1492–1830.* New Haven, CT: Yale University Press, 2006.

Eltis, David. *Economic Growth and the Ending of the Transatlantic Slave Trade.* New York: Oxford University Press, 1987.

———. *The Rise of African Slavery in the Americas.* Cambridge, UK: Cambridge University Press, 2000.

Farrow, Anne, Joel Lang, et al. *Complicity: How the North Promoted, Prolonged, and Profited from Slavery.* New York: Ballantine Books, 2005.

Field, Edward, ed. *State of Rhode Island and Providence Plantations at the End of the Century: A History.* Boston: Mason Publishing Company, 1902.

Fogel, Robert William, and Stanley L. Engerman. *Time on the Cross: The Economics of American Negro Slavery.* Boston: Little, Brown and Company, 1974.

Foner, Laura, and Eugene D. Genovese. *Slavery in the New World: A Reader in Comparative History.* Englewood-Cliffs, NJ: Prentice Hall, 1969.

Fowler, William M., Jr. *William Ellery: A Rhode Island Politico and Lord of Admiralty.* Metuchen, NJ: Scarecrow Press, Inc., 1973.

Franklin, Jameson J. *Privateering and Piracy in the Colonial Period Illustrative Documents.* New York: Macmillan Company, 1923.

Goodrich, Reverend Charles A. *Lives of the Signers to the Declaration of Independence.* New York: William Reed & Co., 1856.

Gorée, Richard Harrison. *Gorée Island, Island of No Return: Saga of the Signarés.* Mount Clemens, MI: Gold Leaf Press, 1992.

Goslinga, Cornelis. *A Short History of the Netherlands Antilles and Surinam*. The Hague, 1979.

Goslinga, Marian. *A Bibliography of the Caribbean*. Lanham, MD: Scarecrow Press, Inc., 1996.

Greene, Lorenzo Johnston. *Studies in History: The Negro in Colonial New England, 1620–1776*. New York: Columbia University Press, 1942.

Grossman, George S. *The Spirit of American Law*. Boulder, CO: Westview Press, 2000.

Hall, Neville A.T. *Slave Society in the Danish West Indies*. Baltimore, MD: Johns Hopkins University Press, 1992.

Haskins, James, and Kathleen Benson. *Bound for America: The Forced Migration of Africans to the New World*. New York: Lothrop, Lee and Shepard, 1999.

Hedges, James B. *The Browns of Providence Plantations: The Nineteenth Century*. Providence, RI: Brown University Press, 1968.

Higman, B.W. *Slave Populations of the British Caribbean, 1807–1834*. Kingston: Press University of the West Indies, 1995.

Howe, George. *Mount Hope: A New England Chronicle*. New York: Viking Press, 1959.

Howe, George Locke. *Slaves Cottage*. New York: Coward-McCann, Inc., 1935.

Inikori, Joseph E., and Stanley L. Engerman, eds. *The Atlantic Slave Trade, Effects on Economies, Societies and Peoples in Africa, Americas, and Europe*. Durham, NC: Duke University Press, 1992.

Jameson, John Franklin. *Privateering and Piracy in the Colonial Period*. New York: Macmillan Company, 1923.

Jefferson, Thomas. *The Jefferson Bible: The Life and Morals of Jesus of Nazareth Extracted Textually from the Gospels in Greek, Latin, French & English*. Washington, D.C.: Smithsonian Institute, 2011.

Johnson, Walter. *Soul by Soul: Life Inside the Antebellum Slave Market*. Cambridge, MA: Harvard University Press, 1999.

Jordan, Winthrop D. *White Over Black: American Attitudes Toward the Negro, 1550–1812*. Chapel Hill: University of North Carolina Press, 1968.

Kimball, Gertrude Selwyn. *Providence in Colonial Time*. Boston: Houghton Mifflin Company, 1912.

Klein, Herbert S. *The Atlantic Slave Trade*. Cambridge, UK: Cambridge University Press, 1999.

Kleinman, Joseph, and Eileen Kurtis-Kleinman. *Life on an African Slave Ship*. San Diego, CA: Lucent Books, 2001.

Lepore, Jill. *New York Burning: Liberty, Slavery, and Conspiracy in Eighteenth-Century Manhattan*. New York: Vintage Books, 2005.

Mannix, Daniel P. *A History of the Atlantic Slave Trade: Black Cargoes*. New York: Viking Press, 1962.

McCarthur, Walter. *The Seaman's Contract, 1790–1818*. San Francisco: Originally published in the U.S. Statutes at Large, 1919.

McManus, Edgar J. *Black Bondage in the North*. Syracuse, NY: Syracuse University Press, 1973.

McMillin, James A. *The Final Victims: Foreign Slave Trade to North America, 1783–1810*. Columbia: University of South Carolina Press, 2004.

Melish, Joanne Pope. *Disowning Slavery: Gradual Emancipation and "Race" in New England, 1780–1860*. Ithaca, NY: Cornell University Press, 1998.

Middleton, Alicia Hopton. *Life in Carolina and New England during the Nineteenth Century*. Bristol, RI: privately printed, 1929.

Middleton, Richard. *Colonial America: A History, 1565–1776*. Boston: Blackwell Publishing, 1992.

Munro, Wilfred H. *Tales of an Old Sea Port; A General Sketch of the History of Bristol, Rhode Island*. Princeton, NJ: Princeton University Press, 1917.

Paiewonsky, Isidor. *Eyewitness Accounts of Slavery in the Danish West Indies*. New York: Fordham University Press, 1989.

Palmie, Stephan, ed. *Slave Cultures and the Cultures of Slavery*. Knoxville: University of Tennessee Press, 1995.

Parry, J.H., P.M. Sherlock, et al. *A Short History of the West Indies*. 4th ed. New York: St. Marten's Press, 1987.

Pelton, Robert W. *Men of Destiny, Signers of our Declarations of Independence and our Constitution*. Charleston, SC: Freedom and Liberty Foundation Press, 2012.

Pope-Hennessy, James. *Sins of the Fathers, A Study of the Atlantic Slave Traders, 1441–1807*. New York: Capricorn Books, 1967.

Preston, Howard Willis. *Rhode Island's Historical Background*. Providence, RI: Remington Press, 1933.

Rappleye, Charles. *Sons of Providence: The Brown Brothers, the Slave Trade, and the American Revolution*. New York: Simon and Schuster, 2006.

Rawley, James A., and Stephen D. Behrendt. *The Transatlantic Slave Trade: A History*. Lincoln: University of Nebraska Press, 1981.

Rediker, Marcus. *The Slave Ship*. New York: Viking, 2007.

Reynolds, Edward. *Stand the Storm, A History of the Atlantic Slave Trade*. Chicago: Elephant Paperbacks, 1985.

Rhode Island Historic and Preservation Commission. *Historic and Architectural Resources of Bristol, Rhode Island*. Bristol, RI, 1990.

Risjord, Norman K. *The Early American Party System*. New York: Harper and Row, 1969.

Robinson, Donald L. *Slavery in the Structure of American Politics, 1765–1820*. New York: Harcourt Brace Jovanovich, Inc., 1971.

Schilthamp, J.A., and D. DeSmidt. *Publikaties en Andere Wetten Betrekking Hebbende op [Publications and the Laws Relating to] St. Maarten, St. Eustatius, Saba, 1648/1681–1816*. Amsterdam: S. Emmering, 1979.

Shepherd, Verene, and Hilary Beckles, eds. *Caribbean Slavery in the Atlantic World*. Oxford, UK: James Currey Publishers, 2000.

Soodalter, Ron. *Hanging Captain Gordon.* New York: Atria Books, 2006.

St. Clair, William. *The Door of No Return: The History of Cape Coast Castle and the Atlantic Slave Trade.* New York: Blue Bridge Books, 2007.

Thomas, Hugh. *Cuba, A History.* London: Penguin Books, 1971.

———. *The Slave Trade, The Story of the Atlantic Slave Trade: 1440–1879.* New York: Simon and Schuster, 1997.

Thompson, Charles, OF. *Sketches of Old Bristol.* Providence, RI: Roger Williams Press, 1942.

Thornton, John. *Africa and Africans in the Making of the Atlantic World, 1400–1800.* Cambridge, UK: Cambridge University Press, 1992.

Tomlins, Christopher L., and Bruce H. Mann, eds. *The Many Legalities of Early America.* Chapel Hill: University of North Carolina Press, 2001.

Van Doren Honeyman, A. *The Honeyman Family in Scotland and America, 1548–1908.* Plainfield, IL: Honeyman's Publishing House, 1909.

Weeden, William B. *Economic and Social History of New England, 1620–1789.* Vol. II. New York: Hillary House Publishers, Ltd., 1890.

Winsnes, Selena Axelrod. *Letters on West Africa and the Slave Trade.* New York: Oxford University Press, 1992.

Wood, Peter H. *Black Majority: Negroes in Colonial South Carolina from 1670 through the Stono Rebellion.* New York: W.W. Norton and Company, 1974.

Newspapers

Bristol County Register. "Marine List." July 15, 1809.

Champlin, Jabez. "United States of America, Rhode-Island District." *Newport Herald*, February 3, 1791.

City Gazette. "Charleston, Monday, August 24, 1807." August 24, 1807.

Davis, Paul. "Living Off the Trade: Bristol and the DeWolfs." *Providence Journal*, March 17, 2006.

East Bay Newspapers. "Linden Place Issue." June 15–16, 1988, special edition.

Gallatin, Albert. "Treasury Department." *Bristol County Register,* April 4, 1809.

Newport Herald. "Commentary." February 3, 1791.

Providence Gazette. "James DeWolf Commentary," June 25, 1791.

———. "The Embargo, a Commentary." May 21, 1808.

Rhode-Island American. "Commentary." November 6, 1810.

INDEX

A

Abbot, Joel 122
abolitionist 13, 26, 45, 58, 80, 109, 129
Adams, John 80
Adams, John Q. 122
Amastad 86, 92, 93
American Revolution 20, 26, 44, 87
Andromache 96, 97, 101, 112, 114
Annamaboe 50
antislavery 81

B

ballast 55, 57, 91, 105
banking regulations 51
Bank of Bristol 51, 91, 119, 125, 128
Barbados 93
Barnes, David 75, 104
black cargo 30, 49
Bosworth, Samuel 28, 70
Bradford, William 51, 116
Bristol County Register 108
Brown, John 73, 76, 81

C

Cadiz 92
campaign 73, 80, 84, 110, 119, 120, 123

Caribbean 57, 64, 75, 104, 109
casks 110
cemetery 98, 100, 130
Chances 64
Charleston, South Carolina 14, 90, 105
chattel 27, 33, 129
Christian and D'Wolf 94
Christian, Charles 94
Christiansborg 50
circumvention 80, 81, 120, 122
Claning, Henry 37, 39
Clarke, Charles 105
Clay, Henry 118
Collins, Charles 42, 67, 75, 84, 85,
    103, 119, 120
Common Sense 87
confiscation 58
Congregational Church 21, 59, 60
Continental Congress 26, 69
cooper 49
counting house 55
Cranston, Jonathon 26

D

Danish Burgher 75
Declaration of Independence 26, 69
de Graaf, Johannes 34

deposition, Rhode Island 23, 24, 26, 27, 37, 39, 40
deposition, West Indies 39, 40, 41, 42
DeWolf, Abigail 16, 21
DeWolf, Adjua 92, 97, 98, 129
DeWolf, Charles 75, 76
DeWolf, George 90, 110, 123, 124
DeWolf, Henry 94
DeWolf, James, Jr., "Gentleman Jim" 94
DeWolf, John 36, 50, 51, 86, 109
DeWolf, Levi 62, 67, 86
DeWolf, Lydia 60, 64
DeWolf, Mark Anthony 15, 59, 124
DeWolf, Nancy Ann 98, 103
DeWolf, Pauledore 92, 97, 98, 99, 129
DeWolf, William 75
Dickinson, John 100
Dutch 32
dysentery 47

E

Ellery, Christopher 69, 86, 120
Ellery, William 17, 24, 68, 75, 85, 120
embargo 108
Empresa Estate 125
enslaved 129

F

Federalist Party 81, 84
Florida 66, 109
foreign flag 107
foreign port 58, 104, 114
French 115

G

Gaillard, John 118
Ghana 50
Gold Coast 50, 96
Golden Rock 32, 34
Gorton, Thomas 26
granite 55, 57, 81
Griswold, Alexander V. 127
Guinea-Bissau 50

H

Hamilton, Paul 108
Harvard 68
Havana 23, 50, 62, 66, 88, 96, 106, 109, 112, 119, 122, 125
Herrero, Joseph Dolores 110
hogsheads 20, 49, 51, 56, 93
Honeyman, Judith 98
House of Representatives 73, 116, 123, 127
Howell, David 104

I

Indians 75, 77
insurance policy 30, 58, 61, 67

J

Jay, John 27, 37, 44
Jefferson, Thomas 84, 93
Judge Jay 37
Juno 65, 71, 73

K

kidnapped 46, 92, 130
King, Rufus 69

L

latitude 66
Lavinia 93
leeward 48
longitude 66
Lucy 75, 76, 77

M

Macdonough 110, 111, 112
Madison, James 13, 108
Manchester, Isaac 36, 37, 41, 42
manifest 57, 92, 93, 97, 104, 106, 112, 118
Mantonell, Juan Jose 92
Marchant, Henry 28, 42
Mariana Estate 125

Matanzas 50, 65, 71, 88, 116, 119
Middle Passage 33, 46, 48, 49, 55, 66,
    67, 73, 86, 96, 112, 122
midnight appointment 80, 85
Minerva 86, 88, 92, 93
molasses 49, 56, 57, 65, 66
Monroe, James 120
Monticello 93
Mount Hope 77
Mount Hope Bank 53
Mount Hope Estate 65
Mount Hope Insurance 58

N

Nagle, David 64
Nancy 28
Negro 26, 27, 81, 86, 115, 119
New Hope Estate 65
Nueva Esperanza Estate 65

P

Paine, Thomas 87
Peck, William 23, 28, 42
Petri, Christian 36
piracy 58
politics 14, 17, 31, 42, 69, 84, 94, 120
Polly 23, 24, 26, 27, 36, 42
Potter, Simeon 15, 46, 70

Q

Quaker 45, 59, 61

R

Ranger 64
Remitance 116
Republican 85, 86, 87, 104
Republican ideology 84
Republican Party 85
Rufus, John W. 109
rum distilleries 46, 51
Runnels, Johannes 35

S

Sally 66, 90
Savannah, Georgia 14, 42
Semiramis 66, 67
Slocum, Charles 67, 75, 111
smallpox 39, 47
Smith, John 115
Sons of Liberty 69
Spain 92, 104, 109, 110, 115, 119
Spanish colors 90, 110, 114
Spanish navy 115
St. Croix 62, 64
St. Eustatius 32, 35, 41
St. Michael's Church 16
Stockman, Isaac 37, 39
Stork 65
St. Thomas 32, 40, 41, 42, 64, 66, 75, 86
Stuart, Archibald 85
surveyor 70, 75, 76, 77, 106, 111

T

Thomas Jefferson 85
Three Sisters 101, 104, 105
Tories 44, 84, 87
trafficking 15, 17, 49, 67, 93, 105, 116
transient 35, 37

U

U.S. Navy 109

V

vertically integrated empire 9, 49, 94

W

warehouse 55, 57, 75, 81, 128
Warren, Russell 20
Washington, D.C. 86, 122
Washington, George 26, 69, 85
wharf estate 57, 128
Wilson, Oliver James 110
windward 49
Wolcott, Oliver 77

ABOUT THE AUTHOR

A California native, Cynthia Mestad Johnson graduated from Westmont College in Santa Barbara and settled into a successful corporate career. Always taking the time for extensive worldwide travel led her to acquire a passion for American history. She continued her education at California State University–San Marcos, becoming its first female recipient of a graduate degree in history. Her research was subsequently published and sold hundreds of copies, which led to a further desire for "archival treasure hunting." A U.S. history teacher who considers her sons to be her proudest achievements, Cindy loves being active outdoors and lives in Carlsbad with her husband, Bill.

For more information, visit www.dewolfslavetrade.org or e-mail the author at dewolfslavetrade@gmail.com.